JERUSALEM'S GATES

UNCOVER THE BLUEPRINT TO YOUR INTENDED PURPOSE

JERUSALEM'S GATES

UNCOVER THE BLUEPRINT TO YOUR INTENDED PURPOSE

JULIAN GARCIA

Trilogy Christian Publishers A Wholly Owned Subsidiary of Trinity Broadcasting Network 2442 Michelle Drive Tustin, CA 92780

This book is dedicated to the memory of Carlos Valencio Brown and to his mother, Georgia Moore, whose love, generosity and passion to advance the word of truth will forever be commemorated in the words of these pages.

I also dedicate this book to my wife, Lilia Garcia, my children, Jadon, Josiah, and Jillian, my amazing parents, Julian and Celia Garcia, and to my friends, Sandra Buford, Darryl and Patricia Hester, Richard McClain, and Ronnie and Cynthia Raeford. I am eternally grateful to all of you for the sincere and faithful love you have for me. Your support has been invaluable in accomplishing this work, and because of it, countless lives will be greatly blessed with its substance – may God attribute it to your account. I love you all.

Lastly, I want to thank Kathleen Hmura for her generous, editorial contribution to this book. Your fervent work to help me convey God's message, more effectively, was a God-send. Each page emanates your skill and passion for excellence, and it allows each reader a greater reading experience. God bless you, Kathy, as your work will forever be a pleasing memorial to our Lord.

CONNECT WITH US

To share a testimony of this book's impact on your life, please email:

Testimonies@revivingthemessage.org

To book Julian Garcia as a guest speaker for one of your events, please email:

Bookings@revivingthemessage.org

To connect with Reviving The Message Ministry, please visit our website at:

revivingthemessage.org

TABLE OF CONTENTS

PREFACE

After attending a Men's Conference in 2011 themed "Breaking New Ground," I found myself prayerfully asking the question, "What does breaking new ground mean to me?" Behind that question was the anticipation that God was going to bless me greatly, either in my personal life, career, or ministry. Shortly thereafter, the Holy Spirit began to steer my thinking into a new direction as he loudly and clearly spoke to my heart the following statement: "You're breaking new ground for me, and not in a new place, but in the same place."

Because I had been led to believe that God was always looking to bless me in all aspects of my life, I originally interpreted "breaking new ground" to mean a new blessing from God. On top of that, I understood blessings to mostly mean financial increase, material increase, and job promotions. This flawed perspective limited my ability to comprehend what God intended to convey to me. As a result, when I sensed the Holy Spirit say, "You're breaking new ground for me...in the same place," I reverted back to thinking exactly that: a blessing on my job, ministry, or personal life. At that point, I thought I just had to simply wait for his blessings to manifest in those areas of my life.

After a couple of days, I felt strongly compelled to read the book of Nehemiah. I was confident it was the Holy Spirit compelling me to do so. I could sense that God wanted to communicate something to me through that book, and thought to myself, "That shouldn't be too difficult; I've read Nehemiah several times." In fact, I presumed to know what direction the Lord would lead me; after all, I had been saved for twenty years and, I thought my experience of preaching and teaching for fifteen of those twenty years gave me some idea about God's strategies. I believed God wanted to warn me of enemies who would attempt to stop the work God planned to do in my life, just like the ones Nehemiah encountered in Sanballat and Tobiah, who committed themselves to stopping God's work through him.

I took authority over what I perceived as oppositions to my blessings, falling back on that good, old-fashioned standby prayer: "I bind you, Satan, and all opposition now, and come against you with the blood of Jesus!"

How often have we moved ahead of God because we thought we had him figured out and believed we knew what he was going to say or do? This tends to happen more often when a person has worked in ministry for a long time, or has simply been a Christian for years and has heard hundreds of predictable sermons.

On this occasion, the Holy Spirit strongly convicted me, and again turned my attention back to the book of Nehemiah. Once I started reading, I realized that the people of God, although delivered from Babylonian captivity for decades, continued to experience great trouble and disgrace after being restored to their homeland. One of the primary reasons for the trouble and disgrace they experienced was that the walls and gates intended to protect them from enemies, robbers and looters, were either damaged or destroyed since the time of the Babylonian conquest. God used that moment to clarify for me, the great spiritual significance behind Nehemiah's reconstruction of Jerusalem's broken walls and burned gates.

Although I had heard countless messages on Nehemiah's rebuilding project, this time I could perceive that his work had eternal meaning and a specific message that is still relevant today. That's when I realized that "breaking new ground" had nothing to do with God blessing me. Rather, it had everything to do with the body of Christ rebuilding and repairing the eternal message and meaning embedded in Nehemiah's reconstruction project; something that the enemy of our faith has successfully managed to tear down.

What also inclined me to write this book involved something God continuously spoke into my heart, "You will break ground in the same place and repair for me what I have already ordained."

Now, I can honestly say that seldom do I sense God impressing on me any particular message or instruction on my heart so strongly. However, time and experience have taught me to recognize God's voice speaking to me. This was definitely one of those occasions! There existed within his message a great sense of urgency. Because of that urgency, I acknowledged the pressing work that needed to be quickly completed by the body of Christ. In order to better understand what God required of me, I needed to do an in-depth study of the third chapter of Nehemiah.

While I rigorously began unpacking Nehemiah 3, I came across many instances of priceless treasure encapsulated within the Scriptures. The more time I spent in them, the more he revealed to me.

The message behind Nehemiah's work began unfolding like a blueprint or master plan that leads us closer and closer to the heart and mind of God. At the end of my study and research, combined with his illumination and revelation, I understood the message God wants revived and restored by his people today.

The entirety of the message and the priceless material I found on my journey of understanding are captured within the pages of this book, "Jerusalem's Gates: Uncover the Blueprint to Your Intended Purpose."

I pray that the content will embolden you with the purpose and zeal to accomplish the work that Christ has ordained you for - indeed, he is eagerly counting on you to do that very thing! Thank you for embarking on this personalized journey with an open heart to receive a greater understanding of His intentions for your life.

Best Regards,

Julian Garcia, Jr.

INTRODUCTION

In 586 B.C., the third wave of Babylonian attacks against God's people in Judah occurred. The walls surrounding their capital city, Jerusalem, lay broken, their gates burned to the ground along with the expulsion of the people into Babylonian exile. This successful attack was prophesied by the prophet Jeremiah in Jeremiah 25:9-11. God promised that his people would be taken into captivity by Babylon for 70 years as a result of their rebellion against him, his commands; and they also refused to listen to the prophets he sent to call them back through repentance.

Exactly 70 years from the time the first wave of Babylonian attacks occurred against Judah, Persia's King Cyrus the Great, allowed many of the surviving remnant of Judean captives to return to Jerusalem after he conquered Babylon.

In approximately 445 B.C., in the 20th year of the reign of Artaxerxes, King of Persia, Nehemiah inquired about his people who survived the exile and had returned to Jerusalem. Nehemiah, a Judean serving as Artaxerxes's cupbearer, learned from his relative, Hanani, and other men from Judah, about the plight of his people in Jerusalem. He felt moved by this news and decided he must go back and rebuild Jerusalem's walls and gates in order to take away the trouble and disgrace his people faced.

In ancient times, fortified walls were built around important cities to make enemy invasion difficult. If a city felt threatened they had only to shut the giant fortified gates along the walls to close the city and prevent the enemy from entering. This type of defense mechanism helped protect the city, its important structures, and its people from takeover and destruction.

Here, we might want to pause and ask ourselves a rather pertinent question: Did God truly need fortified walls and gates around Jerusalem to protect his people against enemy assaults and invasion?

Filled with countless stories of Israel's deliverance from enemies more powerful than they, the Old Testament offers many accounts describing the miraculous signs and wonders God used to help Israel conquer them. Normally outnumbered by well-established nations with more sophisticated weaponry and military skills, they experienced tremendous victories every time God intervened to help them.

What's more, when many of these victories occurred, Israel had not yet settled in their own land or weren't encircled with walls to protect them or gates to enclose them. One could conclude that God did not need Nehemiah to rebuild the destroyed walls and burned gates of Jerusalem since he had proven time after time his ability to protect his people supernaturally. In fact, one could surmise that God's ability to supernaturally protect Israel without any walls and gates would have effectually sent a 'hands-off' message to anyone trying to oppose his people, and thus, prevent Judah's trouble and disgrace.

Nonetheless, we can undoubtedly see that Nehemiah's burden came straight from God's heart. So then, why did he give Nehemiah this burden to rebuild the fortified walls and gates around Jerusalem? Could there have been a greater significance, and even a spiritual purpose, for the walls and gates being repaired and rebuilt in Nehemiah chapter 3?

To better answer this question, we must first understand that the overall theme of the Bible is how YHWH (phonetically pronounced, Yah-way, the Hebrew name of Jehovah God), the Holy God, would vindicate his loving character by making a way for fallen and sinful humanity to be reconciled to himself.

In his infinite wisdom, he put into effect a divine plan that the Apostle Paul liked to call a "mystery". God, throughout millennia, hid this mystery in every Jewish ritual, sacrifice, feast, and holy day found in the Old Testament. He concealed it in the tabernacle and temple, along with all of their furnishings. Every book, story, and prophecy in the Old Testament alludes to the divine mystery. Paul finally gives this glorious mystery a name and called it – Reconciliation!

What exactly does reconciliation mean? Reconciliation comes from a Latin word meaning to bring together again; to re-establish relationship. It comes from the root word "reconcile," meaning to bring into agreement. Reconciliation involves active forgiveness and a face-to-face reuniting of the parties involved.

When Adam and Eve sinned against God, it severed our relationship with him, thus separating humanity from their Creator. This disconnection first resulted in spiritual death; natural death came next and eternal demise eventually followed suit. The Bible makes it clear that sin was the overall, maligned issue separating the Holy God and man. In order to re-establish this relationship, a plan of reconciliation proved necessary to address and resolve this sin issue.

That wouldn't be easy to accomplish. In order to fulfill this plan, our holy and just God had to satisfy his need for justice. Justice required that all who sinned experience both physical death and eternal (spiritual) death. How, then, would God eradicate sin without eternally damning the sinner? Could that even be possible?

And if somehow God could get past that challenge, the plan would then have to make provision for yet another hurdle of the same magnitude. That challenge would be for God to transform the sinful nature of humanity into the holy image of God himself.

Since the Almighty respects free will, he would need the consent of sinful-natured people before transforming them into sanctified, holy children of God. The need to get human consent definitely complicated things but there was not any other way for God to reconcile mankind to himself; allowing man to dwell in his presence forever as did Adam in the Garden of Eden.

Albeit complex and a tall order to fill, God had predestined a magnificent plan with profound detail that accounted for each of his requirements! And, as previously mentioned, God had embedded the specifics of this plan of reconciliation throughout the Old Testament. Once again, God took the opportunity to infuse a profusion of details of this plan of reconciliation in the reconstruction project of the gates and walls of Jerusalem.

However, he not only included how he would reconcile man, but also how he would sanctify them in preparation for Christ's Second Coming; a sanctification necessary for God to achieve his goal of restoring humanity to the perfect state and relationship he once enjoyed with them in the Garden of Eden. There wasn't a more perfect time to foreshadow this plan than during Judah's restoration from captivity to their homeland. With these walls and gates, he pointed to a greater day and a more precious time, when he would make a way for humanity to be reconciled and totally restored to him.

As a result, as the walls and gates Nehemiah rebuilt around Jerusalem were intended to take away Judah's great trouble and disgrace, in like manner, the plan of reconciliation and sanctification they herald is the remedy for removing the great trouble and disgrace humanity experiences as a consequence of sin. Let me reiterate this point again. Within the plan of reconciliation and sanctification revealed in Nehemiah's reconstruction, those struggling with the great problem of sin and the trouble and shame that results from it, would see this issue resolved and taken away.

As we journey through the ancient gates of Jerusalem, you will gain an in-depth understanding of God's plan to reconcile, sanctify, and prepare you and mankind for his Son's Second Coming. You will also conclude the journey having great clarity of God's intended purpose for your life.

Symbolism plays a vital role in each phase of Nehemiah's rebuilding process. We will look carefully at the correlation between Nehemiah's reconstruction and the Christian journey via the abundance of symbolism located in the details of each gate repaired; from the Sheep Gate to the Horse Gate, as well as the messages found in the meanings of the names of those who helped Nehemiah rebuild.

From this, we will be able to clearly understand the Christian journey we are either on, or are being invited to embark upon. From its inception in our lives (when we surrender to Christ) to its desired end (when we hear, 'Well done, good and faithful servant'), we will receive a thorough understanding of the journey in-between. Each gate will navigate us through the Old and New Testament Scriptures to reveal and enhance our comprehension of the specific aspects of the masterful plan that all of God's children should be aware of.

You will be astounded to learn that much of Christ's ministry and acts referenced these same gates. The fact that Christ, during his ministry, frequently alluded to Nehemiah's gates only served to validate their divine message and purpose.

So come, curious and hungry alike; there's more than enough within these covers to elevate us to a fresh and greater understanding of God, his Word, and his purpose for our lives!

Jerusalem's Gates: Uncover the Blueprint to Your Intended Purpose

THE SHEEP GATE

Our journey begins at the Sheep Gate, where Nehemiah's work of reconstruction also began. It was the most vital gate to Judah and man's restoration with God. Without its reparation, all other repairs and work of reconstruction along the wall proved meaningless, as this gate facilitated the daily animal sacrifices God required from his people for the forgiveness of sin. While animal sacrifice may sound cruel, at its core it should be viewed as an act of mercy from God.

The Reason for Sacrifice

For the benefit of every reader, I will lay an important foundation that, for some, will be review, yet will help provide a thorough understanding of the profound significance of this gate.

God first introduced animal sacrifices in the Garden of Eden. Although Scripture does not offer specific details, it becomes easy to see that he sacrificed an animal as an act of mercy, and covered Adam and Eve's nakedness before banishing them from the Garden and his presence (Genesis 3:21).

Genesis chapter 4 introduces us to Cain and Abel, the sons of Adam and Eve. Their story provides more insight into God's disposition of animal sacrifices. When Abel offered a lamb and Cain the fruit of the ground, we learned that Abel's offering found favor with God while Cain's did not. Reading this story in the original Hebrew language affords us a better understanding of these two offerings. This language offers a more precise and clear picture of God's disposition.

In Genesis 4:4-5, "shaah," the Hebrew word for "pleased" or "respect," best illustrates God's feeling, or lack thereof, towards the two different sacrifices. *Shaah* means "to gaze at" or "to gaze about for help." In many instances like this one, this Hebrew word signifies the gaze as a favorable one, with the implication suggesting that one gaze with amazement. In English, "gaze" is defined as "looking steadily and intently, especially in admiration, surprise, or thought."

With this information in mind, we realize that Abel's lamb amazed God and provoked admiration from him, which resulted in God's favorable disposition towards it. In his omniscience, God knew the important role the lamb would play in his future plans, thus evoking feelings of admiration (shaah) on his part. Cain's offering simply failed to draw from him any sense of amazement or admiration. Therefore, there was no reason for God to gaze at it steadily and intently.

In his sovereignty, God chose to enter into a covenant with the Hebrew people, promising to be their God and display his love towards them. It was then that it became more apparent how a lamb would be helpful to him. When God established a covenant with the Hebrew people, he essentially entered into a personal relationship with them. In order to sustain their relationship, he had to address the malignant disease of the soul – sin – which kept God and man separated.

What is sin? In Hebrew, it simply means "to miss the mark," that mark being God's holy standard of righteousness. And as a branch withers and dies when separated from the vine, man's degeneration began the moment Adam and Eve sinned, as their subsequent unrighteousness separated them from God. Along with separation from God came the consequence of death - as God promised Adam. God had warned Adam that once he ate from the forbidden tree, he would "…surely die" (Genesis 2:17). This set precedence for the repercussions faced by all who would sin.

The Bible further solidifies this point in Romans 6:23 (KJV), "… the wages of sin is death…"

A Temporary Fix for Sin

How then could the holy God establish a covenant with sinful people, who, according to his standard, deserved death? With the help of sheep and other animals, a solution became possible.

God fully displayed their help in a very symbolic ritual he designed and called Atonement – or *kaphar* in Hebrew. *Kaphar* literally means "to cover over." It allowed God's anger, caused by sin, to be pacified and allowed him to look at his people favorably.

Therefore, atonement made amends and reparation for sins possible, its concept best explained by God himself in Leviticus 17:11:

> *For the life of the body is in its blood. I have given you the blood on the altar to purify you, making you right with the LORD. It is the blood, given in exchange for a life, that makes purification possible. (NLT)*

In short, animal sacrifices represented transferring the sins of the people to an innocent animal that would be sacrificed instead of the sinner. This demonstrated the conditional forgiveness of the sinner, as their sins were symbolically removed; the punishment of sin satisfied God's justice and wrath. What an act of mercy on the part of God to refrain from executing the punishment of death upon the sinner who deserved it, and instead executing the judgment of death on the sacrificed animal! This showed the people that by virtue of shed blood, they would be forgiven, purified and saved! A merciful act of God, this symbolic substitution allowed the Lord to remain in relationship with his people.

The types and conditions of the animals presented for sacrifice were also important to God. He considered some animals clean, or acceptable, and others unclean, or unacceptable for sacrifice (Leviticus 11). Among the animals that were clean and acceptable for sacrifice were sheep, which were also the symbol for sacrifice, along with oxen, rams, goats, heifers, and turtledoves.

Among other factors, the occasion or cause for any particular sacrifice determined what kind of animal was used. Yet, the one uncompromising mandate God required of all animals to be presented on the altar was that they be without "spot or blemish", meaning without sickness or physical defect.[1]

Ephesians 5:25-27 helps us understand that spots and blemishes, or sicknesses and defects, are a spiritual representation of sin. Outside of a divine ritual, God did not despise a sick or defective animal, or God would have commanded his people to rid themselves of all "spotted" or "blemished" animals. But the moment an animal was introduced to a divinely ordained ritual, like sacrifice, of which the whole had symbolic, spiritual meaning, the sickness and defects of that animal immediately took on the spiritual meaning of sin. At that moment, such animals were useless and became counterproductive since what represented sin could not atone for, or repair, the offense of sin with a holy God. In fact, God viewed presenting any spotted or blemished animals during this spiritual ritual with great displeasure; the act was offensive and contemptible to him.

As we read the Scriptures, we also learn that sacrifices were presented for different reasons and at different times, the most important being on the Day of Atonement when all the sins of God's people, as a whole, were symbolically removed.[2] That particular sacrifice to remove the sins of the entire community only occurred once a year and it was conducted by the High Priest, the highest-ranking religious leader. The community's life and relationship with God was completely dependent on the atoning sacrifice and it being acceptable to God.

Other opportunities for sacrifices included the evening and morning sacrifices which took place on a daily basis. People also offered sacrifices for other various reasons. Some might have chosen to honor God with worship, and others made a vow, committing

---

1 Examples of this requirement are found in Leviticus 1:3, 10; 3:1; and 4:3
2 You can read more about this amazing ceremony in Leviticus 16

themselves to a specific course of action. Other choices might have included seeking counsel, wanting to become ceremonially clean from a skin disease or from giving birth. On each occasion, sins had to be addressed first through the act of sacrifice before approaching God. But no sacrifice had more at stake for the community as a whole than the atoning sacrifice presented on the solemn Day of Atonement.

Judah's process for sacrifice established

Before the Babylonian destruction of Judah, the latter's system for offering sacrifices, especially the annual atoning sacrifice, was well established; the four elements needed for a fully successful ritual were present and functional: the Sheep Gate, the gate where the animals for sacrifice entered the city; the Temple, where the offering was presented; a High Priest, the religious leader designated by God to present the atoning sacrifice; and lastly, the sacrifice, an animal for sacrifice, often sheep, hence the name of the gate they entered the city, the Sheep Gate.

The people brought their animals for sacrifice through the Sheep Gate and, as long as the animal did not appear to be sick or defective, it had no difficulty advancing to the Temple. There, the priest offered it for a sacrifice on the brazen altar located in the Temple's courtyard. Again, only the High Priest (the chief religious leader) offered the atoning sacrifice for the entire community on the most holy day of the year– The Day of Atonement.

Again, all these sacrifices enabled God *to cover over* the sins of the people, either, individually, or as a community, and continue to accept them as his own. For this reason, God's process for restoring relationship with mankind necessitated the practice of putting atonement first, the function of the Sheep Gate. Therefore, when Nehemiah set out to rebuild the walls and gates of Jerusalem, it proved fitting that he started with the Sheep Gate of Jerusalem. Without it, the people would have been restored to their land, but not to their God, thus remaining in a continuous state of great trouble and disgrace, spiritually. With this foundation laid, we can now move on to understand the wonderful revelation of this gate and how Christ validated it.

Eliashib's Reconstruction a Clue to a Greater Act of God

Then Eliashib the high priest and his priestly colleagues arose and built the Sheep Gate. They dedicated it, and erected its doors, working as far as the Tower of the Hundred and the Tower of Hananel.

(Nehemiah 3:1)

Because this gate fell under the jurisdiction of priestly responsibilities, it was fitting that Nehemiah appointed Eliashib, the High Priest, to restore it. Eliashib fulfilled prophecy in all of his labor. He also lived up to the meaning of his name, *God will restore!*

Considering that his Hebraic name truly meant "God will restore," we can clearly see what God accomplished with the help of his work. Eliashib restored part of the necessary elements for God and his people to have a fully functional Sheep Gate. Without his work, atonement and relationship with God would not have been possible.

Eliashib's name provides further insight that must be considered. The meaning of his name – *God will restore* – continuously spoke of a future restoration. First, it prophesied about Israel's restoration in the land of Judah. But even after that restoration, Eliashib's name continued to herald the divine message of yet a future restoration of greater proportions!

When studying prophecy, we learn that most prophecies possess both a natural and a spiritual fulfillment. As Eliashib helped Nehemiah rebuild Jerusalem's Sheep Gate, his work foreshadowed and typified the divine work of a future restoration. You see, the sacrifices of animals allowed God to "cover over" sins, like a bandage covers over a wound. But like a bandage that has to be changed repeatedly because of a wound that doesn't heal, animals had to be sacrificed over and over and over again, in order to cover over the unresolved issue of sin. A permanent fix was needed; and God had it. The permanent solution was neither in the repeated animal sacrifices, High Priests, Temple, or the Sheep Gate, but rather, in the hidden message they represented and pointed us to!

For this reason, in Eliashib's work, God provided clues and insight to his God-inspired plan to rebuild a future spiritual Sheep Gate; allowing access to an everlasting atonement for sin, making possible the permanent reconciliation and restoration of man with God! That was the ultimate plan he had all along since Adam and Eve first sinned!

The Sin of the Priests in Malachi

Leading up to Zechariah the priest's encounter with the angel Gabriel in Luke chapter one, God had been silent from heaven for 400 years. Instead of his people moving God towards the greatest act of love the world would ever see through Christ, in love and obedience, it was the extreme opposite.

Let's take a look at a message from God to the priesthood of the time in Malachi 1:6-9. It will help us understand what led to his 400-year silence and separation from his people.

> *A son naturally honors his father and a slave his master. If I am your father, where is mine honor? If I am your master, where is my respect? The LORD who rules over all asks you this, you priests who make light of my name! But you reply, how have we made light of your name? You are offering improper sacrifices on my altar, yet you ask, how have we offended you? By treating the table of the LORD as if it is of no importance! For when you offer blind animals as a sacrifice, is that not wrong? And when you offer the lame and sick, is that not wrong as well? Indeed, try offering them to your gover-*

nor! Will he be pleased with you or show you favor? Asks the LORD who rules over all. But now <u>plead for God's favor that he might be gracious to us</u>. With this kind of offering in your hands, how can he be pleased with you? Asks the LORD who rules over all.

Despite their tendency to backslide and go after other gods, God consistently demonstrated his love for Israel over the centuries. Their final acts of sin and blatant rebellion during Malachi's time, finally put an end to his patience, and he just left them alone. He didn't speak to them for 400 years.

Malachi begins by utterly rebuking the priests and Levites. He informed them of God's emphatic displeasure with their detestable act of presenting blind, lame, and sick animals for sacrifice. Their brazen disrespect proved that they did not love God or care to maintain a relationship with him. They failed to offer acceptable sacrifices to God, well-pleasing sacrifices adequate enough to substitute for their own sins and failures. The fellowship God once enjoyed with his people came to an abrupt halt as he separated himself from them and ordered the temple doors be closed, a symbol of their ended fellowship (Malachi 1:10).

The only glimmer of hope left appeared when Malachi began imploring the priests to urgently cry out to God, fervently asking him to be gracious to them. Chanan, the Hebrew word for "gracious" in this verse, means "to bend or stoop in kindness to an inferior." Another definition reads as "to favor or move to favor by petition." So, Israel's hope rested on that humble petition, earnestly longing for God to once again show them favor and stoop down in kindness to them and be gracious.

The Revelation at Zechariah's House

Four centuries later the Lord stooped down in kindness, finally moving towards Israel and showered them with grace and goodwill. This move proved to be not only favorable for Israel, but for all of humanity! At the Priest Zechariah's house God set the stage for all to understand the favor and kindness he was going to show all mankind. By virtue of the most gracious act he would ever display, God, once again, made a way for man to be in direct communion and relationship with him.

Around 2 B.C. (400 years since Malachi), God found a priest named Zechariah, a man very different from the priests he chastised in the book of Malachi. He and his wife, Elizabeth, also of priestly lineage, "were both righteous before God, walking in all the commandments and ordinances of the Lord blameless" (Luke 1:6).

Both advanced in years, they were never able to conceive, although they continuously cried out to God to bless them with a child. Because of her inability to conceive, Elizabeth felt disgraced (Luke 1:25). However, Elizabeth and her husband still walked upright before God in spite of the humiliation and unanswered prayers.

One day while performing his duties as High Priest, an angel named Gabriel appeared to Zechariah to give him some really great news. Despite their old age, God would cause them to become parents. Elizabeth would conceive a son whom they would name John (Luke 1:13). Six months later, the same angel appeared to Elizabeth's cousin, Mary. She, on the other hand, was very young and had never been with a man. The angel told her she would be overshadowed by the Holy Spirit and would be impregnated supernaturally (Luke 1:35).

In response to this amazing news, Mary immediately set off alone and traveled between 80 to 100 miles to visit her cousin Elizabeth. Mary's visit to her cousin involved so much more than two pregnant women sharing an amazing experience. God divinely orchestrated this event to communicate something so miraculously profound. Take a look at what appears to be a simple verse in Luke 1:40:

And [Mary] entered Zechariah's house and greeted Elizabeth.

We must look at the original language to better understand the powerful message embedded in this statement. The setting of this verse is in Zechariah's house. The two parties present were Mary and Elizabeth. In Hebrew, Zechariah means "Jehovah has remembered." Mary's name in Hebrew means "their rebellion," and Elizabeth's means, "Oath of God."

Can you see the message that God was conveying? After 400 years of silence, he announced his intention to deal with two things that had come to his remembrance – the people's rebellion, and his promise to reconcile and restore them to himself (for more advanced students of the Bible, this reconciliation would be the ultimate fulfillment of God's covenant with Abraham)!

Why would God keep his promise after his people's constant and deliberate rebellion? Upon closer inspection of the Mary and Elizabeth story, we can see that God placed the solutions to this dilemma in their wombs.

Again, Mary's name means, "their rebellion," and the name of Jesus translates as "Jehovah is salvation." So, in spite of their rebellion, God still had a plan to save them. In Elizabeth, which means "oath of God," he placed the child John, whose name in Hebrew means "God is a gracious giver!" This meant that God was going to fulfill his oath, or keep his promise, through his grace.

Remember, Malachi told the priest that the only hope they had of avoiding judgment was for God to be gracious to them. And that's exactly what God declared through the birth of John the Baptist. He reminded us of his gracious nature and his plan to reconcile his people to himself, the fulfillment of his promise! Doesn't that sound familiar, Grace and Salvation? In fact, the verse that follows, Luke 1:41, paints the picture even more clearly.

When Elizabeth heard Mary's greeting, the baby leaped in her womb, and Elizabeth was filled with the Holy Spirit.

John, the forerunner of Christ and a symbol of God's grace, leaped in response to the presence of Jesus, the symbol of salvation. John's gesture indicated from Elizabeth's womb, his acknowledgment of the Messiah's conception, thus heralding God's plan of salvation by grace. John was to prepare the way for Jesus, putting into readiness his gift of salvation. John and Jesus, then, were perfect symbols of grace and salvation and a reminder that grace makes way for salvation. To this point, Paul writes in Ephesians 2:5-9, "by *grace* you are *saved*…lest any man should boast!"

Grace and salvation would flow from the reconstruction of this spiritual Sheep Gate, making it God's first priority.

Christ: The Four Main Elements of the Sheep Gate

Again, as a reminder, the four main elements needed for a fully functional Sheep Gate, consisted of: the *gate* through which the animal for atonement entered; a *High Priest*, the person designated by God allowed to offer the atoning sacrifice; a *Temple*, where the *atoning sacrifice* was offered; and *the sacrifice*, an animal acceptable and suitable to make atonement for the people. In order for Christ, as Savior, to make an eternal, once and for all, atonement on behalf of all mankind, he would have to embody and restore all four elements of the Sheep Gate. Let's see if the Scriptures support this idea.

In John 10:7, Christ revealed that he was "the gate of the sheep" (NIV). He is the only gateway to the Father and no one is able to come to the Father and enter into his presence and into relationship with him but through Christ (John 14:6), the Gate of the Sheep.

In the seventh chapter of Hebrews, the writer described Christ as a High Priest after the order of the divine figure, Melchizedek, who appeared briefly in the fourteenth chapter of Genesis. God ordained this same Jesus, foreshadowed by Eliashib, the High Priest in Nehemiah, to rebuild this spiritual Sheep Gate; acting as the

High Priest, the Messiah was able to offer the atoning sacrifice that allowed man to be reconciled to God.

When the Jewish leaders demanded a sign from Christ that proved he had the right to drive out the money changers from the Temple, he said, "Destroy this temple and in three days I will raise it up…" (John 2:19). What he referred to as the temple was his body (John 2:21) and the disciples remembered Christ saying this after he rose from the dead (v. 22).

Lastly, when John the Baptist recognized Jesus at the Jordan River, he loudly called out to those present to come see "the Lamb of God who takes away the sin of the world" (John 1:20, NKJV). Here, God made known to all mankind that all the sacrifices offered up to this point, only foreshadowed the death of Christ, God's sacrificial lamb. God would present this ultimate offering to himself in order to save the world from their sins. Reminiscent of Abel's offering, this lamb, Jesus, ultimately *helped* the Father reconcile us through his atoning sacrifice on the cross of Calvary!

The truth remains, that the sacrifices required by God in the Mosaic Law, could only provide temporary fixes for the sins of the people. Unable to permanently remove sin, these annual offerings only hinted at the final sacrifice that would take away their transgressions forever. This is exactly what Hebrews 10:1-4; 10-12a; and 14 conveys:

> *For the law possesses a shadow of the good things to come but not the reality itself, and is therefore completely unable, by the same sacrifice offered continually, year after year, to perfect those who come to worship. For otherwise would they not have ceased to be offered, since the worshipers would have been purified once for all and so have no further consciousness of sin? But in those sacrifices there is a reminder of sins year after year. For the blood of bulls and goats cannot take away sins… [But] By [God's] will we have been made holy through the offering of the body of Jesus Christ once for all. And every priest stands*

day after day serving and offering the same sacrifices again and again – sacrifices that can never take away sins. But when this priest [Christ Jesus] had offered one sacrifice for sins for all time... For by one offering he has perfected for all time those who are made holy.

As you can see, Scripture makes it very clear that in Christ, all four elements required for the reparation of the Sheep Gate could be found: the Gate; the Lamb; the High Priest; and the Temple. He would make amends for the sins of the world through his sacrificial death. He completed its reparation by his resurrection and ascension, making permanent forgiveness of sin and reconciliation possible!

The Significance of Jesus at the Pool of Bethesda

During his three and a half year ministry, Christ endeavored tirelessly to reveal this message and convey the reality that reconciliation with God would soon be made possible to all of humanity. He communicated this through teachings, and provided physical analogies that embedded this message through his acts and healings. We can find one such example in the healing of the paralytic, by the Pool of Bethesda, located near the Sheep Gate, as told in John 5:1-15. Interestingly, this Scripture in John is the only place in the New Testament where we can find any mention of the Sheep Gate. Let's read the text:

After this there was a feast of the Jews; and Jesus went up to Jerusalem. Now there is at Jerusalem by the sheep gate a pool, which is called in the Hebrew tongue Bethesda, having five porches. In these lay a great multitude of impotent folk, of blind, lame, paralyzed, waiting for the moving of the water. For an angel went down at a certain season into the pool, and troubled the water: whosoever then first after the troubling of the water stepped in was made whole of whatsoever disease he had. And a certain man was there, which had an infirmity thirty and eight years. When Jesus saw him lie, and knew that he had been now a long time in that case, he saith unto him,

Wilt thou be made whole? The impotent man answered him, Sir, I have no man, when the water is troubled, to put me into the pool: but while I am coming, another steppeth down before me. Jesus saith unto him, Rise, take up thy bed, and walk. And immediately the man was made whole, and took up his bed, and walked: and on the same day was the sabbath. The Jews therefore said unto him that was cured, It is the sabbath day: it is not lawful for thee to carry thy bed. He answered them, He that made me whole, the same said unto me, Take up thy bed, and walk. Then asked they him, What man is that which said unto thee, Take up thy bed, and walk? And he that was healed wist not who it was: for Jesus had conveyed himself away, a multitude being in that place. Afterward Jesus findeth him in the temple, and said unto him, Behold, thou art made whole: sin no more, lest a worse thing come unto thee. The man departed, and told the Jews that it was Jesus, which had made him whole.

On the surface, it may appear that Jesus simply healed a man who had been an invalid for thirty-eight years and proved his power to heal.

We could easily assume that God intended that healing to serve as a testimony for us, that if God healed back then, he could still heal today. Truthfully, this healing proved to be far more significant than that.

As mentioned before, Christ conveyed his messages in different forms. He often used physical analogies, especially in the healings he performed. He intended to elevate our minds through this type of healing - to center on God's heart and intention to restore mankind to himself. This portion of Scripture beautifully illustrates this very thing.

For this reason Christ arrived at the Pool of Bethesda, purposing to convey one of the essential aspects of the divine plan. There, he foreshadowed the grace that God would both demonstrate and make available in order to bring about salvation to the world.

Remember, nothing contains spiritual meaning apart from God's divine purpose, and this story is certainly filled with divine purpose. Let's observe the spiritual implications of this story as we see it through a spiritual lens and keep foremost in mind Jesus' purpose of making reconciliation with God possible.

Allow me to first draw your attention to the word "sheep" as it pertains to the Sheep Gate. In Greek (the original language of the New Testament) the word is *probatikos*, relating to sheep, i.e. a gate through which they were led into Jerusalem. *Probatikos* comes from the word *probaton,* meaning "something that walks forward on four legs, especially sheep." And *probaton* is derived from *probaino,* meaning "to walk forward, i.e. advance." These meanings help us understand that the Sheep Gate operated as a place where sheep moved forward and advanced – it was the place of advancement!

When presenting animal sacrifices to God, the living sacrifice had to travel through the Sheep Gate and advance towards the temple to be offered by the High Priest. How fitting then, that the Sheep Gate functioned as the place of advancement, leading towards the Temple. Sadly, by the Sheep Gate in John 5, advancement proved to be difficult for a great number of disabled people whose conditions prevented them from moving forward. The blind, the lame, and those paralyzed, illustrated the defective sheep God warned against prior to his 400 year period of silence; those that the priests in Malachi allowed access through this gate and deemed worthy enough to be offered on the holy, brazen altar.

Christ's appearance at the Pool of Bethesda, near the Sheep Gate, became a divine moment; the sicknesses and defects of the people there took on spiritual meaning.

As explained earlier, sicknesses and defects represented sin, and in this passage, Christ attempts to elevate our understanding to see how sin kept humanity spiritually blind, lame, and paralyzed. He drew everyone's attention to the issue of sin; the issue that prevented us from advancing into the Temple.

Symbolically, the Temple represented the presence of God and the place of close communion with him, as literally, the Temple functioned as one of the few designated places intended for God to meet with man after Adam's fall in the garden. Another such place can be located in the Tent of Meeting, or Tabernacle, replaced eventually by the Temple, where only the priest communed with God.

Not only did Christ's presence at the Pool of Bethesda remind us of the sin issue, it also revealed the magnificent part of his plan offering resolution for it. Let's explore some of the further details located in this passage that will illuminate God's course of action.

Prior to Christ's appearance at the pool, popular belief held that the waters, once angelically stirred, contained the power to heal anyone who made it in first. Sadly, each troubling produced more feelings of despair than joy since only one person per stirring actually received any sort of healing.

On the other hand, one could not hold the water responsible for this dilemma; the real problem lay in the bodies of those waiting for the waters to be stirred. Their physical infirmities and maladies prevented them from entering the water without some kind of assistance. Because of the impossibleness of the situation, the waters eventually became a source of torment.

Can you imagine being so close to healing and not being able to obtain it? Now imagine thirty-eight years of being so close to a miracle but having your own inability keep you from it.

The healing water at the pool of Bethesda perfectly parallels the Law of Moses; also known as the Law, it contained God's body of divine commands given to the Israelites as a standard of holiness.

Those seeking salvation during this dispensation were compelled to blamelessly follow the exact letter of this law. Galatians 3:18-19 helps shed some light on the similarities between the healing power of the pool and the Law. Read what it says:

> *For if the inheritance is based on the law, it is no longer based on the promise, but God graciously gave it to Abraham through the promise. Why then was the law given? It was added because of transgressions, until the arrival of the descendant [Jesus] to whom the promise had been made. It was administered through angels by an intermediary.*

Just as the responsibility for stirring the waters and empowering them to heal, belonged to an angel, these celestial beings also introduced the Law, offering healing and life for all who could keep it blamelessly.

When this healing at the pool occurred, the people of God lived under the rule of the Law. Since the time Moses descended from his encounter with God on Mount Sinai, until the resurrection of Christ, Israel's success and blessings as a nation were predicated on their obedience in keeping God's statutes contained in the Law. According to the verse above, God administered the law to Moses through angels. More importantly, God promised life for those who blamelessly kept the Law (Leviticus 18:5). And like the stirred waters of the pool, the Law afforded hope to all who could keep it perfectly.

The problem here involved Israel, and more broadly speaking, all of humanity's inability to live to such a standard of righteousness. Sin had dominion over our will and desires, rendering us all powerless in overcoming the appetites of our flesh. Spiritually, we were blind, lame, and paralyzed like the people at the pool; therefore, the Law, introduced as a hope for life to Israel, ended up judging and condemning them instead. Yet, the healing of the man at the pool presented Israel and all of humanity, as well, with a fresh hope!

By purposeful design, Christ addressed the man who had lain there for thirty-eight years and asked him a rather interesting question: "Do you want to be made well?" A peculiar question since Jesus had never inquired this of any other person he had healed. Why this man? Let's take a closer look.

When studying the Greek word for "want" in this verse, we learn that the word translates to "*thelo*," meaning "to desire" or "wanting what is best because someone is ready and willing to act." In this case, Christ did not concern himself with the way things normally worked at the Pool of Bethesda; he didn't care about the stirring of the waters nor did it matter to him that only the first one in would receive their healing. Christ actually introduced us to a new protocol, new rules of conduct belonging to a new covenant that God would establish through the blood of his sacrificed son.

The new protocol would place the weight on a person's *desire* to be made whole as opposed to their ability to do what it takes to become whole. In the case of the paralytic, the only thing that concerned Christ about him centered on whether the man still wanted to be made well after waiting by the pool for the last 38 years.

Imagine the excitement and great anticipation felt by this nameless gentleman upon arriving at the pool thirty-eight years earlier. His inability to enter the pool must have generated some disappointment but I am pretty sure he still felt confident that next year would be his turn to be healed. However, thirty-eight years of failed attempts appeared to have taken a toll on the man's hope, but did it manage to destroy his will and desire for healing?

It appeared obvious that almost four decades of letdowns had weighed on the man's hope. We can tell by the way he answered a "yes" or "no" question with pitiful excuses as to why he continued to remain in the same condition.

After so long, it became easier to simply justify his condition by saying that others would beat him to the water when the waters were stirred because there was no one to help him in. To hope again and confidently express his original desire to be healed had proven pointless and painful over the years. And like this man, who continuously failed to get into the waters because of his own infirmity, Israel, and humanity, were met with constant disappointment and failed attempts to live out God's law blamelessly. This was because our sinful nature proved too strong to overcome in order to achieve God's standard of righteousness, no matter how hard we tried. Nevertheless, aware of this man's failed efforts and decades of constant letdowns, Christ's question still remained, "Do you want to be made well?"

Christ posed the question to the paralytic not only to elicit a response but to also generate a moment of decision.

As the Greek definition suggests, "desire" means wanting what is best because someone is ready and willing to act. Essentially, Christ had made himself available and willing to act and help the man become well, but the paralytic had to determine if he wanted it. Jesus required not only an answer but that a decision be made.

Kadesh-Barnea, a Place of Decision

This brings to mind the years Israel spent wandering in the wilderness after escaping from Egypt. Let's read Deuteronomy 2:14:

> *Now the length of time it took for us to go from Kadesh-Barnea to the crossing of Wadi Zered was thirty-eight years, time for all the military men of that generation to die, just as the Lord had vowed to them.*

The Hebrew people, or Israelites, found themselves in a situation that reminds me of the paralytic. After being delivered from 400 years of Egyptian slavery, God led them into the wilderness with the purpose of taking them to the land he had promised their forefather Abraham and his descendants.

Ironically, the journey from Egypt to Canaan should have only lasted approximately two weeks. While many know that Israel ended up being in the wilderness forty years, this verse specifies that during those thirty-eight years they were unable to advance past the area of Kadesh-Barnea to the crossing that led to the Promised Land. In the beginning, the Hebrews demonstrated a tremendous zeal to reach the Promised Land, but shortly after, their passion waned and they became distracted, murmured and complained against God, and were filled with unbelief; they lost sight of the true God and his Law.

Kadesh-Barnea became a place of decision. Here, God refused to let them advance unless they expressed a desire to surrender, believe him and walk in obedience to his commands. Unfortunately, the people continued to rebel against Yahweh, the God who brought them out of Egypt with mighty signs and wonders; as a result, he drew the proverbial line in the sand and promised that generation they would never advance to the Promised Land.

Like Isreal, the man at the Pool of Bethesda, found himself stuck and unable to advance for thirty-eight years. When Christ showed up, suddenly it became a place of decision - would he accept Christ's offer of help? Did he really want to be made well?

While the man felt reluctant to believe after suffering decades of failure and disappointment, hope still prevailed. Christ, knowing the man's desires, commanded him to rise up, take up his mat, and walk.

Bethesda: The House of Grace

In Aramaic, *Bethesda* means "House of Kindness" or "House of Grace." Here God reminds us of his willingness to stoop down, show humanity kindness, and be a gracious giver, as he had announced at Zechariah's house. This would come in the form of grace – the agent God would bestow on us to restore us back to him. That grace was and would be in the future both an act and an empowering virtue. You see, this gracious act took place in this scenario when Jesus approached the man, unsolicited. He offered him healing and the virtue of grace which empowered him to do what he couldn't do before! This explains why Christ questioned the man about his readiness to be healed. The Father never imposes his will on anyone and would only bestow his gracious act on the individual if he truly desired it and, by their own freewill, allowed it. This new way of being healed promises the right-standing with God so many long for; something they couldn't attain on their own! They can hope again, but now, in the grace of Jesus!

Do you want to receive Jesus as your personal Lord and Savior? Preachers posing this question at the end of service essentially want to know how badly you want to be made well. Christ earnestly wants to save you, to forgive your sins and make you whole but your freewill has to be considered. It's a simple "Yes" or "No" question that sadly, many only respond to with explanations and excuses. You may hear things like, "Well, that means I'll have to stop… [some type of sin]" or "What if I do it and then can't live up to the standards," or "Yeah, but I still like to… [sin]." Again, while Christ longs to remove the sickness of sin, the person's free will must always be considered, as God cannot override it.

The Effect of Grace on a Life

For those reluctant to surrender to Christ because you don't be-lieve you can live up to his standards or you cannot let go of your bondages, I have some good news for you! There is hope! We can see that hope fully displayed through the healing of the man at the pool! You see, Christ introduced God's new way of healing humanity from sin and bringing us back to him; and this takes place by the empowering agent and virtue called Grace! How so? "Charis," the Greek word for grace, means "God's divine influence on the heart and its reflection on the life." At the pool, the power of Christ's command empowered the man to rise up, retrieve his mat, and start walking. The external evidence of Jesus's authority manifested itself in the paralytic's actions -he did just that. Grace will do the same in our lives -- it will provide us with the power to do the will of God - what we certainly couldn't do before. It symbolizes our ability to walk upright or live righteously before God - again, what we couldn't do before.

So a person may say, "But I'm reluctant to commit to Christ because I don't think I'm able to live up to God's standards." Guess what? You can't! But when Christ takes up residence in your heart after you say, "Yes," you will see the results of the Savior's influence in your life! He begins to move upon the heart first, which the Greek word in this context does not refer to the organ, but instead, to the mind, will, desire, and intellect. Once these areas come under the divine influence of the Almighty, phenomenal changes take place in their lives! Why? Because God's grace influences how you mentally process and view the sin you are addicted to, it influences your desire so as to no longer desire that sin, and your willingness to commit that sin changes. Lastly, your lifestyle will reflect the internal influence of grace upon your heart, as you will likely stop committing those sins that once dominated you. Christ demonstrated this very thing at the Pool of Bethesda.

Now notice what the paralytic could do once he received his healing through the empowering virtue of grace. Verse 14 says, "Later Jesus found the man in the Temple..." At long last, the man finally made it to the Temple! Remember, the goal of all sheep intended for sacrifice involved advancing through the Sheep Gate to get to the Temple. There, provided the sheep had no defects, the priests offered them to God as a holy sacrifice.

Because of the divine moment in this case, Christ demonstrated to us the benefits available to those willing to receive the grace of God and be healed of their sins: it allows us to advance to the Temple, or, symbolically, grant us access to the Father's presence. The moment we surrender to God, because Christ died for our sins, we become justified and declared holy; God's influence on our lives leads us to live righteously by the virtue of grace. Hebrews 4:16 confirms this and invites us to "...confidently approach the throne of grace..." and Romans 12:1 admonishes us to present ourselves as living sacrifices, holy and acceptable before God as grace has now empowered us to do!

But just so that we don't get ahead of ourselves and think that grace gives us a license to continue to sin, notice the profound statement Christ made to the man once he found him in the Temple. He said to him, "See, you are well again. Stop sinning or something worse will come upon you" (John 5:14). First, this statement helps us understand that his infirmity had been the product of his sin which makes it all the more clear that Christ approached this man to foreshadow the work of grace; it also raises two important questions: was Christ implying that salvation would be earned by works? And, how does this statement relate to my personal reconciliation?

Is Accountability Works-Based Salvation?

By no means would a person have to work or earn their salvation as was the case before the work of Christ! The process of restoration through grace was perfectly illustrated in the paralytic's experience. Christ circumvented the process that required him making the effort to enter the water and earn his healing: one, because he would never be able to, and two, because Christ showed up to introduce a new way of obtaining salvation and righteousness.

At the cost of being redundant, I will reiterate my earlier comment on the topic of grace to avoid any possible misunderstanding. I also want to ensure that I have provided a clear explanation of grace. We can see in the case of the paralytic, Christ approached the man and demolished the strongholds obstructing his healing. To walk in good health, the invalid had only to respond to Christ's command to get up and walk.

He simply needed to walk by faith in the grace Christ abundantly blessed him with.

A large part of the issue had always been man's inability to obey God's commands; God settled that issue once and for all with grace. He magnanimously furnished the man with the power to be healed which immediately brought him to his feet! Christ then had full right to demand that the man no longer sin since he had empowered him to do what he couldn't do for the last thirty-eight years!

When Christ generously demonstrated his ability to authorize us to overcome sin through grace, he expected and still expects us to turn away from sin. A failure to reject sin would indicate that we no longer desire his healing, and that we no longer feel confident about his ability to make this possible. Does that necessarily mean we turn away from every sin instantly? Or is it a progressive work? Those questions will be addressed later.

However, the question remained, "When would this promised grace be available to mankind?" Eliashib, the High Priest, answers this question in Nehemiah 3:1:

> "*Then Eliashib...Arose and rebuilt the Sheep Gate.*"

The Bible tells us that when Eliashib arose, work on the Sheep Gate commenced. This also indicated the full restoration of the spiritual Sheep Gate after our High Priest, Jesus Christ, rose from the dead.

THE TWO TOWERS

They dedicated it [the Sheep Gate] and erected its doors, working as far as the Tower of the Hundred [some versions say Meah which means "Hundred" in Hebrew] and the Tower of Hananel. (Nehemiah 3:1)

The work of the Sheep Gate led the High Priest and his priestly colleagues to work as far as the two towers mentioned above. The Towers played an extremely significant role in God's plan of reconciliation. Look at the name of the first tower mentioned, the Tower of the Hundred. Eliashib may not have been aware of the great symbolism taking place as his reparation of the Sheep Gate carried over to the Tower of the Hundred. Christ's parable in Luke 15:1-7 offers us a better understanding of the divine connection between the Sheep Gate and the Tower of the Hundred:

Now all the tax collectors and sinners were coming to hear him. But the Pharisees and the experts in the law were complaining, this man welcomes sinners and eats with them. So Jesus told them this parable: Which one of you, if he has a hundred sheep and loses one of them, would not leave the ninety-nine in the pasture and go look for the one that is lost until he finds it?

Then when he has found it, he places it on his shoulders, rejoicing. Returning home, he calls together his friends and neighbors, telling them, Rejoice with me; because I have found my sheep that was lost. I tell you, in the same way there will be more joy in heaven over one sinner who repents than over ninety-nine righteous people who have no need to repent.

It is in Nehemiah 3:1 that an important framework of God's redemptive plan is revealed. It is that at the rebuilding of the spiritual Sheep Gate, by Jesus, through his death, burial and resurrection, the Hundred can be saved. What people could be counted among the "Hundred?" Everyone who would say, "I desire to be made well!" Romans 10:13 (NKJV), says it best: "For whoever calls on the name of the Lord shall be saved." Therefore, the Hundred represents all who say "yes" to Christ, and it implies that no one has to be lost! So again, through his sacrifice, Christ rebuilt the gate that makes atonement for our sins possible; whoever desires to be forgiven of their sins and saved, will be.

The work then moved further along to the second tower, known as Hananel; an edifice vital in helping us better understand how to live godly lives after being made well. While the first chapter says much about how we would be able to live a life that's pleasing to God after being made well, or simply put, receiving salvation, the Tower of Hananel will provide greater insight. Let's take a closer look at the popular story in Genesis 1:1-9:

> *The whole earth had a common language and a common vocabulary. When the people moved eastward, they found a plain in Shinar and settled there. Then they said to one another, "Come, let's make bricks and bake them thoroughly." (They had brick instead of stone and tar instead of mortar.) Then they said, "Come, let's build ourselves a city and a tower with its top in the heavens so that we may make a name for ourselves. Otherwise we will be scattered across the face of the entire earth." But the LORD came down to see the city and the tower that the people had started building. And the LORD said, "If as one people all sharing a common language they have begun to do this, then nothing they plan to do will be beyond them. Come, let's go down and confuse their language so they won't be able to understand each other." So the LORD scattered them from there across the face of the entire earth, and they stopped building the city. That is why its name was called Babel--because there the LORD confused the language of the entire world, and from there the LORD scattered them across the face of the entire earth.*

The Babel experience not only informs us how the earth ended up with so many different languages, but also help us understand the why.

The Scripture clearly states that the people determined to build a tower in an attempt to make a name for themselves; what better way to do it than to build a tower that reached heaven? While this sacred passage does not specify their intent to reach God himself, biblical scholarship teaches us that the people of this period subscribed to the belief that God dwelt among the immediate heavens. So, it makes sense that reaching heaven would make a name for themselves as they would have reached God. Other possible motives for building the tower include a fear of being scattered and a need for protection from devastating disasters such as the flood Noah and his family survived. Either way, they took their salvation into their own hands. They decided to build a tower with the bricks they made rather than use the countless number of God-created stones available to them. Everything about this tower had a human design and imprint. God expressed his displeasure of their project by refusing to allow man to connect heaven and earth with their strength or for humanity to save themselves by their own hand. As a result, God confused them with different languages in order to stymie their plan of connecting earth to God by their own might.

Despite God's obvious dislike of the Babel project, the idea of a tower contained some merit since it aligned with God's plan for reconciliation. Here, God further strengthened his plan to rectify the God/man fracture by adding to his blueprint, the Tower of Hananel, along with the other walls and gates in Jerusalem. Why? Because *Hananel* in Hebrew means "God is gracious!"

Clearly, God used this tower to let us in on his divine plan, making grace the agent responsible for connecting earth to heaven, or man to God. This explains how a tower became a symbol for grace instead of a gate. The more steps you ascend in the tower, the higher you go. In like fashion, God's grace elevates us and enables us to walk upward "toward the mark for the prize of the high calling of God," Philippians 3:14 (KJV).

This also coincides with what happened at the Pool of Bethesda. When Christ bestowed grace on the invalid man, he said, "Rise," and the man got up! Grace will always cause you to rise and walk upright. Those walking in grace cannot continue to live in sin, because it causes you to rise and walk upright. To remain in a lifestyle of sin would mean rejecting God's grace and his help in producing righteousness within us. This very grace compels us to holiness, something the Apostle Paul stressed in his epistle to Titus, his son in the faith.

> *For the grace of God has appeared, bringing salvation to all people. It trains us to reject godless ways and to live self-controlled, upright, and godly lives in the present age, as we wait for the happy fulfillment of our hope in the glorious appearing of our great God and Savior, Jesus Christ. He gave himself for us to set us free from every kind of lawlessness and to purify for himself a people who are truly his, who are eager to do good. (Titus 2:1-14)*

Therefore, every person who surrenders their life to Christ enters through God's spiritual Sheep Gate. The sacrifice of Christ allows for the forgiveness of our sins, making us part of the "hundred" saved sheep at the Tower of the Hundred. No longer lost, we are found; therefore, we now live by the grace, or Hananel, of God, which directs us to a holy and righteous way of life.

Further evidence that the time of grace had come

Nehemiah 3:1 tells us that the gate making possible our atonement had been fully restored at Christ's resurrection from the dead. New Testament Scriptures provide us further evidence that the time of grace, or the Tower of Hananel, had arrived.

Take a close look at what occurred in Acts 1:6-11:

> *So when they had gathered together, they began to ask him, "Lord, is this the time when you are restoring the kingdom to Israel?" He told them, "You are not permitted to know the times or periods that the Father has set by his own authority.*

But you will receive power when the Holy Spirit has come upon you, and you will be my witnesses in Jerusalem, and in all Judea and Samaria, and to the farthest parts of the earth." After he had said this, while they were watching, he was lifted up and a cloud hid him from their sight. As they were still staring into the sky while he was going, suddenly two men in white clothing stood near them and said, "Men of Galilee, why do you stand here looking up into the sky? This same Jesus who has been taken up from you into heaven will come back in the same way you saw him go into heaven."

After his resurrection, Jesus appeared to his disciples over a 40-day period. During his last appearance and conversation with them, something interesting occurred. Right before his disciples' eyes, Christ, like a tower, ascended up from earth to heaven, thereby connecting the two! What exactly happened? God connected earth to heaven by virtue of his gracious act when he gave his son as a ransom for our sin, raising him from the dead, and carrying him to heaven. Consequently, the empowering agent of grace became available for all who would call on the name of the Lord.

Here's proof – when men attempted to save themselves with the Tower of Babel, God stepped in and confused them with different languages. After connecting earth to heaven with Hananel, his tower of grace, God reversed what he did at Babel! In Acts chapter 2:1-11, following the ascension of Jesus, we are given magnificent news:

*Now when the day of Pentecost had come, they were together in one place. Suddenly a sound like a violent wind blowing came from heaven and filled the entire house where they were sitting. And tongues spreading out like a fire appeared to them and came to rest on each one of them. **All of them were filled with the Holy Spirit, and they began to speak in other languages as the Spirit enabled them.** Now there were devout Jews from every nation under heaven residing in Jerusalem. When this sound occurred, a crowd gathered and* *was in confusion, because **each one heard them speaking in his own language.** Completely baffled, they said, "Aren't all these who are speaking Galileans? And how is it that each one of us hears them in our own native language? Parthians, Medes, Elamites, and residents of Mesopotamia, Judea, and Cappadocia, Pontus and the province of Asia, Phrygia and Pamphylia, Egypt and the parts of Libya near Cyrene, and visitors from Rome, both Jews and proselytes, Cretans and Arabs—**we hear them speaking our own languages about the great deeds God has done!**"*

God did a 180 turn in the Book of Acts from what he had done in Genesis, by implementing the use of foreign languages. Empowered by the Holy Spirit, his followers spoke in foreign tongues. Those present on Pentecost expressed amazement at the great deeds of God declared in their own language!

God was declaring, "I have built a tower through Christ that has connected earth to heaven. I have made a way of salvation for all mankind with my mighty right hand. I no longer need man to be confused, but instead, I want everyone to understand and communicate with each other; to know that God has once again been gracious, making a way for all mankind to be reconciled!" Therefore, the same tongues, or languages, he used to confuse mankind in Genesis, he enabled his disciples to speak to eliminate all confusion and have them hear the message of Christ! That same day, 3000 people repented of their sins, were baptized, and became reconciled to the Father!

God's Announcement at the Gate called Beautiful

In the third chapter of Acts, the lame man's healing illustrates beautifully the new era of empowering grace through Christ. At the Pool of Bethesda, Jesus showed us how grace would empower us to walk uprightly and live up to God's standards. The Messiah further added that we could also enter his presence and have communion with God, but all of this would take place at the appointed time. In Acts chapter 3:1-10, God gave humanity a clear sign that the hour of grace had come, and in fact, was available for all who desired it.

> *Now Peter and John were going up to the temple at the time of prayer, at three o'clock in the afternoon. And a man lame from birth was being carried up, who was placed at the temple gate called "the Beautiful Gate" every day so he could beg for money from those going into the temple courts. When he saw Peter and John about to go into the temple courts, he asked them for money. Peter looked directly at him (as did John) and said, "Look at us!"*

> *So the lame man paid attention to them, expecting to receive something from them. But Peter said, "I have no silver or gold, but what I do have I give you. In the name of Jesus Christ the Nazarene, stand up and walk!" Then Peter took hold of him by the right hand and raised him up, and at once the man's feet and ankles were made strong. He jumped up, stood and began walking around, and he entered the temple courts with them, walking and leaping and praising God. All the people saw him walking and praising God, and they recognized him as the man who used to sit and ask for donations at the Beautiful Gate of the temple, and they were filled with astonishment and amazement at what had happened to him.*

A man, lame from birth, relied on the help of others to place him outside the temple gate called "Beautiful" so he could beg for money. Again, in this divine moment, the man's lameness took on the spiritual meaning of sin.

Like him, sin positioned humanity outside of the Temple, unable to enter into the presence of God. Subsequently, without God's grace, we were cast out of His presence, and, like beggars, we searched for something that could compensate for our broken relationship with him. In this man's case, he thought he needed money. But on the day Peter and John went to the Temple, God showed up to address this man and all of humanity who found themselves in this same condition.

Peter demanded the man's attention and said to him, "I don't have silver or gold, but I'll give you what I do have." Then he said something worth noting, "In the name…" Name in Greek means *authority*. In this instance, Peter referenced the authority of Jesus when he said, "In the name [authority] of Jesus." What was Jesus' authority? In the context of everything that occurred leading up to this moment, Peter spoke of the grace authorized by Christ for all who desired it; the grace made available to them through his death, burial, resurrection, and ascension, for all who wanted to be healed of the issue of sin. So, they commanded the man to get up and walk as Christ had done with the paralytic at the Pool of Bethesda, thus symbolizing the arrival of the promised grace.

The Meaning of the Gate Beautiful

To get a clearer picture, we must understand what "Beautiful" means. The Greek word in this text is *horaios*, from which we get the word "hour." It means, "belonging to the right hour or season; timely, that is."

Peter and John proclaimed to this man, and subsequently, to all of humanity, the arrival of the hour and season for the outpouring of grace (1 Peter 1:10-12). The time that the Prophets of old prophesied about—a future day of grace that the Scriptures pointed to—had come! Once again, a lame man physically unable to advance into the temple, symbolically received grace, stood up and walked; no longer disabled—he went jumping and praising God into—the Temple! This man's healing is emblematic of how God, through grace, empowers a person to leave their life of sin and walk uprightly, and restores their access to God's wonderful presence. What better response than to jump and praise God?

In like manner, we found ourselves cast outside the presence of God begging to be saved and continuously seeking to fill our God-shaped void in a myriad of ways. Those willing to surrender their hearts and lives to the loving call of the Shepherd can also experience the same deliverance and joy as did the man at the gate Beautiful!

Remember, God always intended to heal the blind, lame, and paralyzed, symbolizing a fallen humanity in its sinful state. It was sin that prevented mankind from advancing into his presence and enjoying fellowship with him. But from the day the lame man received his healing at the Gate Beautiful until now, it has been the same hour and season of grace. This grace still offers deliverance from sin and advancement into the loving arms of the Father.

Please do not take this hour of grace for granted! Those accepting the blood of Christ for the atonement of their sins have now been reconciled to God through grace. God then takes them to the next gate of his plan, the Fish Gate. There they will understand their God-purpose during this beautiful hour of grace in a refreshing way.

THE FISH GATE

The sons of Hassenaah rebuilt the Fish Gate. They laid its beams and positioned its doors, its bolts, and its bars. (Nehemiah 3:3)

Operating as a gate of transactions, the Fish Gate played a critical role in God's plan of redemption. It led to the fish market in Jerusalem where fishermen brought their catch and sold their fish. This business of buying and selling closely resembles the inner workings of the redemptive process. The term, *agorazó*, the Greek word for redemption, translates to mean "to go to the market and make a purchase." In Revelations 5:9, we read of twenty-four elders and four living creatures singing about Christ, and the song they sing says:

> *You are worthy to take the scroll and to open its seals because you were killed, and at the cost of your own blood you have purchased for God persons from every tribe, language, people, and nation.*

The Bible likens the people's salvation with the act of making a purchase at a market. The verse above refers to Christ as the purchaser. To better understand the analogy of Christ as redeemer, a few points need clarifying; where is the market located and who is he buying from. Basically, who is doing what and where as it pertains to redemption? These answers can be found at the Fish Gate, particularly in the spiritual lessons it offers.

Nehemiah assigned the reconstruction of this gate to the sons of Hassenaah, whose name means "thorny." Hassenaah's meaning will be addressed later but it is important to keep in mind the relationship of the builders – they were brothers, and their relationship is significant to the meaning of this gate.

The Symbolism of the Fish

To help guide our perspective throughout this gate, let's explore the symbolism of the fish as it is revealed in the book of the prophet Ezekiel 47:1-12:

Then he brought me back to the entrance of the temple. I noticed that water was flowing from under the threshold of the temple toward the east (for the temple faced east). The water was flowing down from under the right side of the temple, from south of the altar. He led me out by way of the north gate and brought me around the outside of the outer gate that faces toward the east; I noticed that the water was trickling out from the south side. When the man went out toward the east with a measuring line in his hand, he measured 1,750 feet, and then he led me through water, which was ankle deep. Again he measured 1,750 feet and led me through the water, which was now knee deep. Once more he measured 1,750 feet and led me through the water, which was waist deep. Again he measured 1,750 and it was a river I could not cross, for the water had risen; it was deep enough to swim in, a river that could not be crossed. He said to me, "Son of man, have you seen this?" Then he led me back to the bank of the river. When I had returned, I noticed a vast number of trees on the banks of the river, on both sides. He said to me, "These waters go out toward the eastern region and flow down into the Arabah; when they enter the Dead Sea, where the sea is stagnant, the waters become fresh.

Every living creature which swarms where the river flows will live; there will be many fish, for these waters flow there. It will become fresh and everything will live where the river flows. Fishermen will stand beside it; from Engedi to En-eglaim they will spread nets. They will catch many kinds of fish, like the fish of the Great Sea. But its swamps and its marshes will not become fresh; they will remain salty. On both sides of the river's banks, every kind of tree will grow for food. Their leaves will not wither nor will their fruit fail, but they will bear fruit every month, because their water source flows from the sanctuary. Their fruit will be for food and their leaves for healing."

This prophecy by Ezekiel spoke of a day when living water would extend out from the Temple, God's residence on earth; it would flow eastward through the Arabah Desert and into the Dead Sea. The Arabah Desert was a sterile valley that led to the lowest part of the earth's surface, the Dead Sea, where no creature could live because of its great salt concentration. The healing water flowing from God's presence represented what we now call the "Gospel message" or the "good news"; wonderful tidings proclaiming God's reconciliation of man to himself through the atoning blood of his son, Jesus. Wherever this message of the Gospel would go, it would bring healing and life, regardless of how dead and fruitless the environment would be! In fact, this message would reach down to the lowest and most dead places and produce God's life and fruitfulness.

What else did this prophecy reveal? It depicted fishermen casting their nets by the banks of the newly formed river, catching *many kinds* of fish.

In Revelation, the people purchased by Christ's blood hail from "every language, tribe, people, and nation." Ezekiel's "many kinds of fish" and Revelation's different kinds of people represent the same thing - people from different nations and ethnicities. Ezekiel's prophecy concerning the fish in the fishermen's nets and the others purchased through Christ's blood in Revelation, indicate those who would make up the citizens of God's kingdom. A further investigation into the meaning of fish enables us to better understand why God would use the metaphor of fish when referring to these people.

Dag, the Hebrew word for fish, derived from dagah, means "a fish as prolific" (producing offspring in abundance); "to move rapidly, to spawn, i.e. become numerous." God used the symbol of fish because the manner in which fish reproduce provides the perfect depiction of how he intends his kingdom to grow – rapidly and numerously!

As for the fishermen depicted in Ezekiel's prophecy, they would eventually become "fishers of men," catching many souls in their Kingdom nets via the Gospel message. Christ understood this perfectly. When the Messiah initiated his ministry, he understood that his role as the High Priest in the plan of reconciliation involved rebuilding the Sheep Gate in order to make forgiveness of sin possible and grace available. He also knew that the duty of reconstructing the Fish Gate belonged to the brotherhood, as evidenced by the sons of Hassenaah who rebuilt the Fish Gate in Nehemiah 3.

With this knowledge, Christ made a stop at the Sea of Galilee, as related in Matthew chapter 4:18-22, to call his first disciples.

> As he was walking by the Sea of Galilee he saw **two brothers,** Simon (called Peter) and Andrew his brother, **casting a net** into the sea *(for they were fishermen). He said to them, "Follow me, and I will **turn you into fishers of people.**" They left their nets immediately and followed him. Going on from there he saw **two other brothers,** James the son of Zebedee and John his brother, in a boat with Zebedee their father, **mending their nets**, then he called them. They immediately left the boat and their father and followed him.*

And just as brothers rebuilt the Fish Gate in the book of Nehemiah, Christ appointed pairs of brothers to help him rebuild the spiritual Fish Gate. Who better to do it than fishermen? These fishermen understood the concepts of this occupation, which allowed them to leverage those concepts for Kingdom growth as they became fishers of men and the gospel message their net.

While the first two pairs of disciples shared an actual biological brotherhood, all future followers of Christ would share that relationship spiritually (Romans 8:29) and would also be made responsible for growing the Kingdom through evangelism (Mark 16:15).

As told in the Book of Acts, the disciples finally produced rapid and numerous growth for the Kingdom of God starting from the day of Pentecost and on. On Pentecost day, 3000 people got saved with 5,000 more being added in a later chapter of the book of Acts. During that time, the Kingdom continued to grow daily

How did they become so effective? Well, Christ used three and a half years of ministry to educate the brotherhood about the necessary components of an evangelism powerful enough to change the world. The disciples focused on those components from the Day of Pentecost onward, and grew the Kingdom as Christ intended. His message and example must continue to be followed in our current generation if we want to witness evangelism executed God's way.

Lesson #1: Partnership

The first lesson we will explore is found in Luke 9:1-6:

> *After Jesus called his twelve together, he gave them power and authority over all demons and to cure diseases, and he sent them to proclaim the kingdom of God and to heal the sick. He said to them, "Take nothing for your journey—no staff, no bag, no bread, no money, and do not take an extra tunic. Whatever house you enter, stay there until you leave the area. Wherever they do not receive you, as you leave that town, shake the dust off your feet as a testimony against them." Then they departed and went throughout the villages, proclaiming the good news and healing people everywhere.*

Luke provides us with a list of instructions Christ gave his disciples when he sent them out to preach in different places he would later visit. The Gospel of Mark 6:7-13, also draws our attention to an additional detail worth noting:

> *Jesus called the twelve and began to send them out two by two. He gave them authority over unclean spirits. He instructed them to take nothing for the journey except a staff—no bread, no bag, no money in their belts—and to put on sandals but not to wear two tunics. He said to them, "Wherever you enter a house, stay there until you leave the area. If a place will not welcome you or listen to you, as you go out from there, shake the dust off your feet as a testimony against them." So they went out and preached that all should repent. They cast out many demons and anointed many sick people with oil and healed them.*

Mark adds that Christ sent his disciples out two by two. This pairing taught them the powerful role partnership played in Kingdom growth; hence, the brotherhood. Luke's detailed account of Christ's selection of his first disciples further highlights the importance of partnership and provides us answers as to why it would be necessary.

> *Now Jesus was standing by the Lake of Gennesaret, and the crowd was pressing around him to hear the word of God. He saw two boats by the lake, but the fishermen had gotten out of them and were washing their nets. He got into one of the boats, which was Simon's, and asked him to put out a little way from the shore. Then Jesus sat down and taught the crowds from the boat. When he had finished speaking, he said to Simon, "Put out into the deep water and lower your nets for a catch." Simon answered, "Master, we worked hard all night and caught nothing! But at your word I will lower the nets." When they had done this, they caught so many fish that their nets started to tear. So they motioned to their partners in the other boat to come and help them. And they came and filled both boats, so that they were about to sink. But when Simon Peter saw it, he fell down at Jesus' knees, saying, "Go away from me, Lord,*

for I am a sinful man!" For Peter and all who were with him were astonished at the catch of fish that they had taken, and so were James and John, Zebedee's sons, who were Simon's business partners.

Then Jesus said to Simon, "Do not be afraid; from now on you will be catching people." So when they had brought their boats to shore, they left everything and followed him. (Luke 5:1-11)

To begin dissecting this passage, we must realize the divinity of this moment. Since Christ's primary intention for choosing this location centered on choosing disciples he would use to grow God's kingdom, we need to pay close attention to the various instances of symbolism found in this text.

Here, Christ used Peter's fishing boat to bring to life his "fisher of men" metaphor. This proved to be emblematic of their future – they would be preaching and teaching the Word of God.

Further symbolism can be seen in the Lord's decision to send Peter out to fish once more, although fishing all night had yielded them no catch whatsoever. In obedience to Christ's command to go deeper, Peter and his brother Andrew went back out to cast their nets and that time caught such an abundance of fish that their nets started to tear. After catching such a massive haul of fish, Peter and Andrew signaled their need for help to James and John, their partners in another boat. Between the four of them, they loaded so many fish into both vessels, that each one began to sink! We find, embedded within this analogy, an important lesson making us aware of the impossibility of adding great numbers to the Kingdom of God without the benefit of partnership!

Alone, Peter and Andrew didn't have enough room in their boat to support their catch. Their efforts would have been in vain and their bounty lost had they not had partners they could call and rely on. The truth still holds that one person, or any one ministry, doesn't have the capability, resources, strength, space, or capacity to manage God's intended growth for the Kingdom.

This partnership illustrated in Luke 5, involves much more than our present understanding and practice of this principle. The partnership discussed here entails more than sending an offering to our favorite ministry once a month. No! This partnership requires more than just our money; it also requires our time, energy, skills, talents, resources, prayers, intellect, etc. When we truly understand Kingdom growth and it genuinely becomes our personal and ministry goal, it humbles us to realize that our mission is bigger than us; it puts things into proper perspective. We don't have enough on our own to accomplish it.

When we forgo partnership with other Christians or ministries and our mission becomes more centered on simply growing church membership without Kingdom purpose or accomplishing personal agendas that don't glorify God, we lose our godly perspective and open the door to all kinds of evil works; fleshly motives and sin set in. This prevents Kingdom growth as God intended. Such an approach falls short of God's standard and will never yield rapid and numerous growth. But those who leverage the beautiful design of partnership will discover the beauty of miraculous multiplication as long as they keep with the other lessons we'll learn from the Fish Gate!

Lesson #2: You feed them!

Let's go to Luke 9:10-15 to learn the second lesson:

> *When the apostles returned, they told Jesus everything they had done. Then he took them with him and they withdrew privately to a town called Bethsaida. But when the crowds found out, they followed him. He welcomed them, spoke to them about the kingdom of God, and cured those who needed healing. Now the day began to draw to a close, so the twelve came and said to Jesus, "Send the crowd away, so they can go into the surrounding villages and countryside and find lodg-*

ing and food, because we are in an isolated place."

But he said to them, "You give them something to eat." They replied, "We have no more than five loaves and two fish – unless we go and buy food for all these people."(Now about five thousand men were there.) Then he said to his disciples, "Have them sit down in groups of about fifty each." So they did as Jesus directed, and the people all sat down.

Upon the disciples' return from outreaching two by two, they met with Christ to tell him all about it. Once the people heard that Jesus was near, a conference of at least 5,000 people soon clustered around to hear Jesus preach on the Kingdom of God. When evening approached, the disciples suggested that Jesus let the people go find food and lodging. Christ answered them, "You give them something to eat." Christ's response made it clear that the responsibility to feed the people belonged to the disciples, thus illustrating the next principle of growth.

The reference to feeding meant much more than just physical, it also had a spiritual connotation. In fact, God began teaching us this principal from the time of Jesus' birth. Luke 2:6-12 reads:

While they were there, the time came for her [Mary] to deliver her child [Jesus]. And she gave birth to her firstborn son and wrapped him in strips of cloth and laid him in a manger, because there was no place for them in the inn. Now there were shepherds nearby living out in the field, keeping guard over their flock by night. An angel of the Lord appeared to them, and the glory of the Lord shone around them, and they were absolutely terrified.

But the angel said to them, "Do not be afraid! For I proclaim to you good news that brings great joy to all the people. Today your Savior is born in the city of David. He is Christ the Lord. This will be a sign for you: You will find a baby wrapped in strips of cloth and lying in a manger."

As we discussed in chapter one, God had stonewalled Israel for 400 years; no prophetic word from heaven, no visions or dreams - absolutely no communication whatsoever. As a result, the people suffered spiritual deprivation on a massive scale, desperately hungering for a word from God. After many years passed, God broke the prolonged silence by sending his son Jesus, who called himself the bread sent down from heaven (John 6:51).

The birth of Jesus, by purposeful design, took place in a manger as there was no room for Mary at the inn. Why? God was more interested in making a declaration. With no room at the inn, Mary gave birth to baby Jesus in the only room available—a stable. She wrapped him in swaddling clothes and placed him in a manger. Then, angels appeared to the shepherds nearby, keeping guard over their sheep. They triumphantly announced the birth of the Savior and Messiah whom the shepherds would find in a manger.

To the average person who doesn't deal with livestock, a manger may not have significant meaning, but these shepherds fully appreciated the importance of this "food box", a place from which the sheep ate their food or drank water. What then was the great news? God finally spoke to his people, Israel, broadcasting to the shepherds and leaders that after 400 years of misery, things were finally looking up. It was a symbolic message from the angels saying, "Hey, we know you've been starving for the past four centuries, but now there's plenty to eat. There's food in the food box for you to feed the sheep once again! You will now eat the living Bread sent down from Heaven, the Word of God you all have been starving for! Shepherds, feed the sheep!"

Furthermore, after Christ's resurrection, he appeared to his disciples and spoke privately with Peter:

> *Then when they had finished breakfast, Jesus said to Simon Peter, "Simon, son of John, do you love me more than these do?" He replied, "Yes, Lord, you know I love you." Jesus told him, "Feed my lambs." Jesus said a second time, "Simon, son of John,*

do you love me?" He replied, "Yes, Lord; you know I love you."
Jesus told him, "Shepherd my sheep." Jesus said a third time,
"Simon, son of John, do you love me?" Peter was distressed that
Jesus asked him a third time, "Do you love me?" And said,
"Lord, you know everything. You know that I love you." Jesus
replied, "Feed my sheep." (John 21:15-17)

The overall message is clear—it is our responsibility to feed the sheep. When Christ was born, the announcement from heaven was, "Shepherds, feed my sheep." In the middle of Christ's ministry, he makes the disciples aware that the responsibility to feed the people belonged to them. And lastly, before ascending to heaven, Christ asked Peter to prove his love for him by feeding his sheep.

This explains why Paul the apostle made it clear to Timothy in 2 Timothy 2:15 (Modern English Version), "Study to show yourself approved by God, a workman who need not be ashamed, rightly dividing the word of truth," because it would be his responsibility to teach its truths, which is what it means to feed God's sheep!

Today, humanity still finds itself at the mercy of God's people diligently studying the Scriptures, and are dependent upon their ability to both learn them accurately and teach them effectively.

When Christ said to his disciples, "The harvest truly is plenteous, but the laborers are few" (Matthew 9:37, KJV), he used a word for "laborer" that has a figurative meaning of *teacher*. During that time, the majority of the religious leaders continuously misled the people with misrepresentations and false teachings of the Torah. The people, ready to hear and receive the truth of the word of God, could not due to the teachers' lack of willingness and skill to "rightly divide the word of truth." Think about it, most of the work we do in the Kingdom involves teaching the Scriptures in one form or another. Through sustained, sound teachings, many come to believe in Christ and are saved (Romans 10:14), grow in Christ (1Peter 2:2), and then become teachers of Christ and his word, as well.

Conversely, as addressed in the Scriptures throughout the New Testament, erroneous teachings give birth to deception and apostasy. This happens because most people will take on the perspective of their teachers and church leaders and believe the Scriptures according to their teachers' belief system.

As teachers of the Word, one of the greatest deceptions we often face concerns the issue of church growth; the more people attending and getting involved in our ministries must mean more growth taking place. On many occasions, we'll find large churches filled with people uneducated in the Word of God; who have not experienced internal transformation, as they have not been fed the true milk of the Word. The teachers may quote Scriptures, but take them out of context, without the proper meaning or understanding. In like manner, while many people attended the synagogues in Bible times, true Kingdom growth did not occur because of erroneous teachings. However, things changed on the Day of Pentecost. Peter preached the true message and meaning of the Scriptures, which convicted hearts and generated faith; lives were surrendered and Kingdom growth began to take place.

Again, both, the people's personal growth and Kingdom growth depend on the brotherhood feeding the sheep by preaching and teaching the truth of the Word of God. Christ, our High Priest, assumed responsibility for the Sheep Gate, but we, the brothers and sisters in Christ, must take charge of the Fish Gate, meaning evangelism and kingdom growth.

Lesson #3: The Fish must work with the Bread

As we further read in Luke 9:16-17, we learn what Christ did to help the disciples feed the multitude:

> *Then he took the five loaves and the two fish, and looking up to heaven, he gave thanks and broke them. He gave them to the disciples to set before the crowd. They all ate and were satisfied, and what was left over was picked up--twelve baskets of broken pieces.*

Once again, a divine moment occurred and another lesson learned. The bread sent from heaven most certainly represented Jesus (John 6). The two fish symbolized the disciples, just returning from their mission trip where they preached two-by-two! Christ took the bread and the fish and blessed them. No greater unity exists than that of the "Bread" and the "Fish"; the working of these two elements together is sufficient to feed hungry multitudes - or what the multitude of 5000 represented in the Bible - a spiritually starved humanity in need of God! In fact, Christ blessed the coming together of the two and at that moment the bread and fish multiplied to satisfy the hunger of thousands. In that significant moment, Christ not only conveyed to his disciples their call and responsibility to feed the hungry humanity, but he emphasized the importance of including the bread in all that they did in order to bear fruit and produce the kingdom growth God intended.

Let's take a look at another significant Scripture that helps drive this point: John 21:1-9. This occasion took place after Christ's resurrection; over the next forty days, he appeared to his disciples to assure them that he was indeed, very much alive. Christ purposed to not only reassure and instill confidence in his followers but also to provide them with the necessary, final instructions that helped them to effectively continue forward. The following account illustrates one such occasion.

> *After this Jesus revealed himself again to the disciples by the Sea of Tiberias. Now this is how he did so. Simon Peter, Thomas (called Didymus), Nathanael (who was from Cana in Galilee), the sons of Zebedee, and two other disciples of his were together. Simon Peter told them, "I am going fishing." "We will go with you," they replied. They went out and got into the boat, but that night they caught nothing. When it was already very early morning, Jesus stood on the beach, but the disciples did not know that it was Jesus. So Jesus said to them, "Children, you don't have any fish, do you?" They replied, "No." He told them, "Throw your net on the right side of the boat,*

and you will find some." So they threw the net, and were not able to pull it in because of the large number of fish. Then the disciple whom Jesus loved said to Peter, "It is the Lord!" So Simon Peter, when he heard that it was the Lord, tucked in his outer garment (for he had nothing on underneath it), and plunged into the sea. Meanwhile the other disciples came with the boat, dragging the net full of fish, for they were not far from land, only about a hundred yards. When they got out on the beach, they saw a charcoal fire ready with a fish placed on it, and bread.

After Christ's death, the disciples found themselves discouraged, confused, and defeated. Several had left businesses and all they had to follow Jesus. Perplexed and depressed, Peter decided to return to his safe haven, fishing, and six other disciples accompanied him. Peter, the professional fisherman, and the disciples fished all night, but failed to catch a single fish. Clearly, it wasn't because fish weren't nearby, as we can gather from the Scriptures. By purposeful design, the disciples caught nothing all night. This experience takes us back to Luke 5, when Peter, Andrew, James, and John first encountered Jesus, the day he called them to follow him. As on that previous occasion, Christ set them up for a miraculous catch that continues to provide valuable lessons for Christian living today. In the morning, Christ asked them if they had caught anything. Not recognizing him, they simply responded, "No." However, at Christ's command, they flung their nets over the right side of the vessel which immediately filled up with an exceedingly large number of fish.

Jesus made it clear that all their efforts throughout the night were ineffective because they fished without the Bread (Christ); but in the morning, when the Fish (the disciples) began to work with the Bread, they caught more fish than their nets could hold. His past experience fresh in his mind, Peter quickly made his way to the shore knowing it was the Lord. There, he found Christ preparing breakfast for all of them, a meal of bread and fish purposely designed to remind them of the necessity to work in conjunction with Christ.

What does it mean today to work without the Bread when it comes to fishing for men or feeding the sheep? It simply means that any efforts we make in evangelism or in producing maturity in the church that is devoid of Christ is futile. There are many examples in today's church where we will find messages being preached that are devoid of Christ, his teachings, his true intentions and determinations. Although many are presented as gospel, sound doctrine, or even, divine revelation, when investigated deeper, the divine substance is missing, and the evidence is apparent in the lives that have a form of godliness, but have not experienced true transformation.

Furthermore, despite our clever marketing tactics and strategies to grow our ministries, if Christ's message of reconciliation and his true doctrines are lacking, attendance may grow, but it doesn't mean the people have been caught in the net of the Kingdom, nor does it translate to Kingdom growth.

That is why we have an abundance of excited and motivated church folk, today, eager to achieve their purposes in life but still are not subject to the rule, reign, and authority of Christ in their lives. Why? Many times it's because they encountered charismatic people with a compelling, motivational message that cited Scriptures from the Bible, albeit erroneously, but were never presented with the true Bread, his true message, doctrines, or intentions that would produce fruit in them.

Final Lessons for Rebuilding the Spiritual Fish Gate

Let's read the rest of what happened once Peter and the disciples made it to shore where Christ was waiting, in John 21:10-14:

Jesus said, "Bring some of the fish you have just now caught."
So Simon Peter went aboard and pulled the net to shore. It

was full of large fish, one hundred fifty-three, but although there were so many, the net was not torn. "Come, have breakfast," Jesus said. But none of the disciples dared to ask him, "Who are you?" Because they knew it was the Lord. Jesus came and took the bread and gave it to them, and did the same with the fish. This was now the third time Jesus was revealed to the disciples after he was raised from the dead.

Immediately upon getting to shore, no discussion took place regarding the death of Christ, or even his resurrection. Christ simply made a statement that would lead to the final lessons – he requested that the fish be brought to him.

Since Christ already had fish grilling for breakfast, what can we safely extrapolate from his request for more fish? Jesus obviously intended to cut and clean these additional fish before setting them on the coals to cook. What makes this mundane, ordinary activity so extraordinary?

To enhance the perspective of this point, we must reference Isaiah 6:1-7:

In the year of King Uzziah's death, I saw the sovereign master seated on a high, elevated throne. The hem of his robe filled the temple. Seraphs stood over him; each one had six wings. With two wings they covered their faces, with two they covered their feet, and they used the remaining two to fly. They called out to one another, "Holy, holy, holy is the LORD who commands armies! His majestic splendor fills the entire earth!" The sound of their voices shook the door frames, and the temple was filled with smoke. I said, "Too bad for me! I am destroyed, for my lips are contaminated by sin, and I live among people whose lips are contaminated by sin. My eyes have seen the king, the LORD who commands armies." But then one of the seraphs flew toward me. In his hand was a hot coal he had taken from the altar with tongs. He touched my mouth with it and said, "Look, this coal has touched your lips. Your evil is removed;

your sin is forgiven."

In this text, the prophet Isaiah shared about his encounter with the holy and glorious presence of the Lord. What an awe-inspiring moment! While standing in this shekinah atmosphere, his mind could focus only on one thing - his sin. He felt doomed because of it. Being a man of unclean lips, how could God ever consider Isaiah to be worthy enough to declare the oracles of God?

God didn't go out of his way to caress and massage Isaiah's sin-consciousness, nor did he attempt to make him feel worthy enough despite his sin. No! Instead, God found a resolution for Isaiah's sin. Removing the coal from the burning altar with a pair of tongs, the angel carried it over to Isaiah and touched his lips; this gracious act, a symbol of purification and sanctification, removed his sin and granted him the forgiveness he so sorely desired. Then God asked a question:

> *I heard the voice of the sovereign master say, "Whom will I send? Who will go on our behalf?" I answered, "Here I am, send me!" He said, "Go and tell these people..."(Isaiah 6:8-9a)*

Apparently, God had a message he needed to communicate with his people, Israel. He required a spokesman and Isaiah volunteered. Although a sinful man, God found Isaiah to be useful and provided the necessary atonement for his fallen nature; taking a hot coal, the Angel touched Isaiah's lips, the cause of his sin. Expectations of doom reinforced his feelings of unworthiness. Once God resolved Isaiah's sin issue, he qualified Isaiah to go out and speak on his behalf. So, the same person who moments before felt unworthy and doomed, felt useful and willing to help God as soon as grace was extended to him and his sin issue was resolved. This is the same idea Christ was communicating on the shore of the Sea of Galilee in John 21.

With fish already cooking on the coals, Christ asked for additional fish, surely to have enough to feed all the disciples. However, these fish also needed to be cut, cleaned and set on the coals, the embers similar to those used to sanctify Isaiah. The coals figuratively sent a message to the disciples: Whenever they made a "catch" of humanity, they needed to bring these fish to Christ, leaving the process of sanctification to him. Only God himself, possessed the power to purify and sanctify them.

The Holy Spirit engages in a process called sanctification, producing a holy character in an individual, gradually lessening their desire to sin. Those submitting to this process learn to develop a godly character, reflecting the righteous nature of their Father - they become holy! Once a person's character undergoes a certain degree of purification, they learn to consistently die to the flesh, or renounce the desires of their sinful nature. Those reaching this level have died to themselves and learn to work with the Bread, providing sustenance for those needing food; remember, only <u>dead</u> fish can feed the hungry– like the boy's two dead fish used to feed the 5,000. That process has not changed today.

As Christians, we should be actively seeking out the lost in order to bring them to Christ so they can be saved. With his blood, Christ purchases them, forgives them, and commits himself to purifying and sanctifying their lives. Once purified, or having reached a certain level of sanctification, that person becomes useful for the work of the Lord. God uses the sons of "thorns" in much the same way he used the sons of Hassenaah to rebuild the Fish Gate in Nehemiah; the word "Hassenaah" meaning "thorny."

Symbolic of a curse, these sharp annoyances (thorns) continue to act as painful reminders that God cursed the ground after Adam and Eve sinned. Born under the curse of sin and death, all of humanity is in need to be brought to the Fish Gate to be redeemed. That is why we need God's fishermen, the brotherhood he has created, to be committed to evangelism so Jesus will have a catch of people he can redeem, forgive and sanctify.

The Major Challenge Encountered at the Fish Gate

However, keep this in mind: in the process of rebuilding the Fish Gate of Jerusalem, Nehemiah encountered an issue.

But their town leaders would not assist with the work of their master. (Nehemiah 3:5b)

There was a group of people who refused to help with the work. In all the reconstruction and reparation of Jerusalem's gates and walls, this issue happened only at the Fish Gate, the gate symbolic for evangelism and kingdom work and growth. Today, the two areas where the church often finds trouble gaining strong commitment from Christians are: the in-depth study of Scripture and evangelism.

Many people get excited about the possibility of preaching, singing, or sharing their different gifts in the church. However, when it comes to studying the Scriptures or going out and spreading the Gospel of Christ, the enthusiasm needed to passionately sustain such initiatives, tends to wane. As a result, many studies have found that Christianity is losing ground to the growth of other religions in the U.S. and abroad.

I hope this chapter increases your understanding of the important role you play in helping God grow his Kingdom. This work falls under your jurisdiction. If we don't do it, no one else will! It is our time, now, to take on the burden of Christ to reconcile man to God and take our nets and go make a catch that Christ can buy back!

THE OLD GATE

Once we have been reconciled to God through the atoning blood of Jesus, the Father commits to sanctify our lives and prepare us for Christ's Second Coming. Then, we'll be totally restored to the image of God and the perfect fellowship he intended to have with mankind as demonstrated in the Garden of Eden. Sanctification prepares us for that day, a process symbolized by most of the remaining gates Nehemiah rebuilt. Jerusalem's gates function as phases of the spiritual journey that every saint must traverse on our way to that Great Day, the return of Jesus Christ. The Old Gate marks the first stop in our journey of sanctification.

Joiada son of Paseah and Meshullam son of Besodeiah worked on the Jeshanah [Old] Gate. They laid its beams and positioned its doors, its bolts, and its bars. (Nehemiah 3:6)

Let me begin by first providing you important information about this gate so that you can thoroughly grasp its significance. Among scholars, this gate acted as one of the more controversial doorways among the twelve gates that surrounded Jerusalem during Nehemiah's time. The controversy revolves around both the name and the designation it was given as its final location in modern times. Some scholars hold the position the name, "Old," supports the belief that this was indeed, the oldest gate among the twelve; others agree that the name "Old" referred to the old city, Jerusalem, formerly known as Salem.

A level of mystery surrounds this gate, many arguing over its exact location. Some scholars insist it lay in the northern sector of Jerusalem, others the South, the East, or the West. Great minds struggle with this topic, often their thinking loses clarity and never arrives at the truth. Of course, God alone knows the answer to this. And to emphasize this point, God used Joiada, whose name happens to mean in Hebrew "Jehovah knows," as one of the builders. This serves as a constant reminder that, what scholars may not know, the Lord knows!

Like the Old Gate, many aspects of God often leave men baffled because they can't quite figure them out—but God knows them and graciously reveals them to those who, in good conscience, set their hearts to understand them.

Incomprehensible definitely defines the manner in which God develops a personal relationship with those desiring it. However, God offers us great insight into this mystery at the Old Gate.

Joiada and Meshullum will introduce us to two agents that God uses in our spiritual Old Gate to draw us into a personal relationship with him. Also, at this stage of our Christian journey, God transforms us and alters our walk in a profound way.

The Question of Faith

Allow me to continue our study by addressing a question that all Christians will be presented with at some point in their lives:

How can you believe in a God you cannot see?

Christians are often met with ridicule by the secular world, mostly due to Christians' inability to provide tangible, scientific evidence that supports their belief in God. Because of common misconceptions regarding the subject of faith, many non-believers view our faith as a crutch for the weak-minded. Many such misconstructions arise from incorrect explanations regarding the definition and working components of faith.

For example, someone choosing to place their "faith" in a dictionary to better understand the meaning of this term, may come across a definition listing faith as a strong or unshakeable belief in something, without proof or evidence. Heavily relied upon search engines define faith as a strong belief in God or in the doctrines of religion, <u>based on spiritual apprehension rather than proof</u>.

Should these definitions prove to be true, criticism of believers would be warranted; indeed, it would be appropriate to call Christians narrow-minded and brainwashed.

But those wanting to obtain a true understanding of Christian faith, must look to the Bible, as well as the original language in which the word "faith" was used in Scripture. Hebrews 11:1 makes a strong declaration of faith that we must not ignore. Look closely at what it states:

> *Now faith is the substance of things hoped for, the evidence of things not seen. (KJV)*

All of Scripture, including the verse above, completely contradict the definitions of faith provided to us by the secular world. When we investigate the word "faith" in its Greek form and definition, the word translates as *pistis*, meaning "persuasion." The verb form of this word, *peitho* means "to convince." This helps us understand that our Christian belief in God comes from being persuaded by God in such a convincing way that we are left with an overwhelming confidence of his existence.

The Scripture above takes it a step further and states that this faith consists of both substance and evidence. Such an assertion leaves no room for our faith to be based on subjectivity or assumptions, because evidence has to be based on a body of facts that ascertain something to be definitively true. The question becomes, "How does faith become substance and evidence?" The answer can be found within the study of the Old Gate.

The Significance of Joiada

Let's begin with Joiada, as he will reveal to us the first agent God uses to convince, transform, and develop a closer relationship with an individual. As previously noted, Joiada means "Jehovah knows."

His father was Paseah, meaning "limping."

During my personal study on the Old Gate, I found myself at a loss with these two individuals, not really understanding what God wanted to convey with this relationship. It seemed obvious that as Paseah fathered Joidada, there also existed a close association between "limping" and the "Lord knows."

This had me baffled. What connection could there possibly be between "Jehovah knows" and a limper? As I pondered this, the precious Holy Spirit quickened my spirit, prompting me to read Genesis 32. Take a look at what verses 24-32 say:

> *And Jacob was left alone; and there wrestled a man with him until the breaking of the day. And when he saw that he prevailed not against him, he touched the hollow of his thigh; and the hollow of Jacob's thigh was out of joint, as he wrestled with him. And he said, "Let me go, for the day breaks." And he said, "I will not let you go, except you bless me." And he said to him, "What is your name?" And he said, "Jacob." And he said, "Your name will be called no more Jacob, but Israel: for as a prince have you power with God and with men, and have prevailed." And Jacob asked him, and said, "Tell me, I pray you, your name." And he said, "Why is it that you do ask after my name?" And he blessed him there. (AKJ)*

I want to stop here on verse 29 for a moment in order to point out a few things. Jacob, also known as a conniver and deceiver, was the second son of Isaac, one of the patriarchs of Israel. He was soon to reconcile with his older brother Esau, Isaac's firstborn, from whom he had stolen the patriarchal blessing.

The patriarchal blessing was designated for the firstborn son, and among other things, it ensured the firstborn the largest portion of inheritance; it also promised great stature among his family and bloodline.

When Jacob's father, Isaac, was old and nearly blind, Jacob disguised himself as Esau, while Esau was out hunting, and asked his father to bless him with the irreversible blessing of the firstborn son. Isaac, firmly believing Jacob to be Esau, laid his hand on his younger son and blessed him. Upon learning what had occurred, Esau became so enraged to the point that he determined to kill Jacob. As a result, Jacob's mother, Rebekah, sent him to a distant land, to her brother Laban's house, in order to protect him from Esau and spare his life. Decades later, Jacob traveled back to his Father's house and would reunite with his brother; which brings us back to Jacob's present predicament. This same journey situated him in the desert where he had the above encounter with a man who wrestled with him throughout the night. This was no ordinary man he wrestled, but rather, a divine one; a wrestling match ordained and designated by God to complete a work in Jacob.

Church revivals often use this particular passage of Scripture as an example of being persistent in prayer, not letting go of God until *we cause him* to bless us. Generally speaking, these prayers involve materialistic desires holding no eternal value. However, the original text makes it clear that Jacob held no interest in such blessings. In fact, he never asked the man to give him anything. Instead, Jacob insisted the man bless him before letting him go. Well then, what kind of blessing was Jacob demanding from the man?

The original meaning and context help us understand that the word "bless" in this passage means to submit, or surrender. For those that don't understand wrestling or Mixed Martial Arts (MMA), when you're in a submission hold, your opponent won't release you until you lose consciousness or signal your desire to surrender through a tap, also known as, a tap-out. This was the same thing.

In essence, Jacob declared to this man, *I won't let you go until you surrender, or submit to me* – tap out, per se. The man did just that – he submitted, Jacob won, and Jacob let the man go. The man then told Jacob that he had fought with God and with men and had prevailed against both.

And while Jacob had, metaphorically, wrestled against his brother, his father, and his treacherous uncle Laban, this occasion proved to be quite exceptional. Jacob discovered he had wrestled a divine being – who symbolized God himself.

At the end of the match, the Angel informed Jacob that he would no longer be called "Jacob," but "Israel." The reason for this can be found by examining the Hebrew origin of the term "wrestle," which translated, means "be-dust." Not commonly used, "be-dust" simply means to cover with dust. This makes sense in this particular situation as both men wrestling in the dirt-filled desert were bound to be covered with dust. We need to appreciate the significance of this definition and how it impacts our understanding of this text.

To better understand the significance of this dust-filled wrestling match God initiated with Jacob, we must look at a few scriptures. First, let's take a look at Isaiah 43:1.

> *Now, this is what the Lord says, the one who created you, O Jacob, and formed you, O Israel: "Don't be afraid, for I will protect you. I call you by name, you are mine." (NET)*

It's important to note that Jacob was created while Israel was formed. Now Genesis 2:7:

> *And the LORD God formed man of the dust of the ground, and breathed into his nostrils the breath of life; and man became a living soul. (KJV)*

Just as God formed man from the dust of the earth, God took that old, conniving, deceitful Jacob and covered him with dust all night long in that desert as they wrestled, and formed him anew! No longer would he be that old, degenerate individual, but now he would have a new nature and a new identity.

Notice what happened in the remainder of the passage, Genesis 32:30-32, when "Jacob" was changed to "Israel":

> So Jacob named the place Peniel, explaining, "Certainly I have seen God face to face and have survived." The sun rose over him as he crossed over Penuel, but he was limping because of his hip. That is why to this day the Israelites do not eat the sinew which is attached to the socket of the hip, because he struck the socket of Jacob's hip near the attached sinew. (NET)

After this amazing experience, Jacob "wrestled" with the mind-blowing realization that he had personally encountered God. He said, "I have seen God face to face, and my life is preserved." Jacob called the place Peniel, which means "face of God." God used this divinely crafted experience to change Jacob's identity and he never walked the same again.

Jehovah tailor-made the exact experience needed to transform Jacob into a truly changed man. This man had wrestled all of his life to get ahead, whether with his father, brother, or uncle, so God chose a wrestling match that guaranteed to reach him.

Even though Jacob had no scientific evidence verifying his encounter with God, his changed identity and limp indicated that something remarkable had definitely happened; an inward and outward reminder of his brush with the presence of El Shaddai were left as a personal sign for him. The same goes for all who accept the atoning blood of Christ for the forgiveness of sin and wholeheartedly desire to know God more intimately.

For those of us who receive his forgiveness and seek to know him, God customizes an experience with each one of us to convince us that He Is – meaning that he exists. He changes our identity, our walk, or lifestyle, and our perspective.

The experience at the Old Gate cannot be taught, but can only be revealed by God himself through situations, circumstances, and individual experiences and encounters. All experiences differ from one another because of the personal nature of each experience; God custom-fits each encounter to effectively reach the person it is intended for. And while most people will never actually see God in physical form on earth, the overall objective of these customized experiences is that our hearts and minds can see, and are able to grasp and understand, that we have witnessed—His Face—the divine attributes, features, and characteristics of God.

We all need to look back on all of our personally tailor-made experiences with our Creator in order to pinpoint the specific encounters or appointments with God that led us to where we are spiritually today. What happened to create within you a deep conviction about the existence of God? And while there may be no direct scientific evidence or pictures of the experience to prove it to learned men, these brushes with his presence compelled you to passionately testify about that experience with heartfelt conviction. You can easily recall the place, day, time, or time period your conversion took place, joyfully recounting the event, or events, in great detail. In fact, this same experience(s) will help you maintain your faith in God during great times of trial, when everything else seems obscure.

That was exactly the purpose of that experience—God intended to develop in you a faith in him so strong that nothing could dissuade you of his existence – it was your Old Gate experience!

I would like you to consider another factor. When God revealed himself to Jacob, Jacob was alone. No one witnessed this wrestling match. Why? I propose that God set his sights on Jacob alone because he personally needed this encounter and subsequent transformation. Your experience was not customized for you to create proof for the world, but to provide proof to you; to persuade and convince you, to transform you, and change your walk, and to become a substance and evidence for you.

Like many scholars who question and debate the Old Gate, the secular world may challenge your testimony, the enemy working in them to sow seeds of doubt as to what you experienced. But, stand firm and confident knowing that God has graciously revealed himself to you.

Remember, just as in Daniel's case, God can exculsively reveal himself to a person, when that person has set their heart on earnestly seeking him.

Only I, Daniel, saw the vision; the men who were with me did not see it. On the contrary, they were overcome with fright and ran away to hide. I alone was left to see this great vision. (Daniel 10:7-8a)

In Daniel chapter 10, the prophet Daniel wrote about the revelation God gave him of a divine being who most scholars agree to be a vision of the glorified Christ. What a moment of great insight and revelation! Daniel saw the glorified Messiah before his eventual appearance on earth. As the above scripture reveals, only Daniel saw the vision, and Daniel 10:12 explains God's willingness to reveal such a great vision to Daniel.

Then he [an angel] said to me, "Don't be afraid, Daniel, for from the very first day you applied your mind to understand and to humble yourself before your God, your words were heard. I have come in response to your words."

Daniel is widely known as a man who sought after God wholeheartedly. He humbled himself before God and desired to gain insight into the things that only Jehovah knew. As a result, the Father revealed them to Daniel. Those accompanying Daniel, missed out on this divine moment. While we could make strong assumptions as to why God did not reveal himself to those accompanying Daniel, what we do know with certainty is that Daniel lived an honorable and devoted life before the Lord. We would be wise to model his lifestyle and devotion, and direct our hearts to know God intimately.

The Significance of Meshullum

Nehemiah names Meshullam, son of Besodeiah, as the second person God used to repair the Old Gate. Meshullam in Hebrew means "ally." What does the term, "ally", actually mean? One definition lists it as a helper, someone fighting right alongside of you in battle. In our journey through the Old Gate, God provides us with an ally to help accomplish the purpose of the gate - that is, to know God personally and intimately; however, God doesn't give us just any ordinary ally.

Through Besodeiah, God allows us considerable discernment into the identity of this ally. *Besodeiah* in Hebrew means "from the counsel of Jehovah." Who makes up the counsel of Jehovah? It is Himself (the Father), the Son, and the Holy Spirit! To determine which member from the counsel Meshullam represents, let's look at the following verses from the Gospel of John (AKJ).

And I will pray the Father, and he shall give you another Comforter, that he may abide with you for ever; Even the Spirit of truth; whom the world cannot receive, because it sees him not, neither knows him: but you know him; for he dwells with you, and shall be in you. (14:16-17)

These things have I spoken to you, being yet present with you. But the Comforter, which is the Holy Ghost, whom the Father will send in my name, he shall teach you all things, and bring all things to your remembrance, whatever I have said to you. (14:25-26)

But when the Comforter is come, whom I will send to you from the Father, even the Spirit of truth, which proceeds from the Father, he shall testify of me: (15:26)

However, when he, the Spirit of truth, is come, he will guide you into all truth: for he shall not speak of himself; but whatever he shall hear, that shall he speak: and he will show you things to come. He shall glorify me: for he shall receive of mine, and shall show it to you. (16:13-14)

Notice the word "comforter" in the above verses - it refers to the Spirit of God. While it was appropriately translated "comforter" in this version of the Scriptures, other versions use "advocate" or "helper."

From the original Greek language, biblical scholars use the Greek word "parakletos" in these texts to represent an advocate, comforter, and guess what else? A helper! Therefore, the scriptures above reveal to us that the Holy Spirit sent down from God acts as our comforter, advocate, and helper, or ally! One of the functions of our ally is to guide us into all truth. In Greek, "to guide" means "to conduct." Therefore, the Holy Spirit conducts us into all truth, as the Scripture above denotes.

Furthermore, our divine ally, or helper, sent down from the counsel of God, also helps lead us into an intimate relationship with God by opening our spiritual understanding, causing us to know God and his ways. 1 Corinthians 2:5-14 (NKJV) has something to say about the matter:

> *...your faith should not be in the wisdom of men but in the power of God. However, we speak wisdom among those who are mature, yet not the wisdom of this age, who are coming to nothing. But we speak the wisdom of God in a mystery, the hidden wisdom which God ordained before the ages for our glory, which none of the rulers of this age knew; for had they known, they would not have crucified the Lord of glory. But as it is written: Eye has not seen, nor ear heard, nor have entered into the heart of man the things which God has prepared for those who love Him. But God has revealed them to us through His Spirit. For the Spirit searches all things, yes, the deep things of God. For what man knows the things of a man except the spirit of the man which is in him? Even so no one knows the things of God except the Spirit of God. Now we have received, not the spirit of the world, but the Spirit who*

Julian Garcia   85

is from God, that we might know the things that have been freely given to us by God. These things we also speak, not in words which man's wisdom teaches but which the Holy Spirit teaches, comparing spiritual things with spiritual. But the natural man does not receive the things of the Spirit of God, for they are foolishness to; nor can he know them, because they are spiritually discerned.

The world (meaning the natural, secular man) cannot see, receive, or know him. But those filled with the Holy Spirit after their encounter with the living God, gain great insight into God and the deep spiritual things that pertain to him. Paul made known to us that our faith experience at the Old Gate cannot be determined by man's wisdom but by the demonstration of the Spirit and of power.

The Holy Spirit, our comforter, advocate, helper, teacher, guide, leads, teaches, and reveals to us the mysteries of God. Without the Spirit of God we cannot know the things pertaining to God - his love, character, mysteries, and determinations.

Christians seeking a closer, more intimate walk with God, will find him at the Old Gate. There, you will also be filled with the Holy Spirit, an ally who will also accompany and lead you through the rest of the sanctifying journey God has prepared for all of his children.

The next phase of the plan he'll lead you to from your Old Gate is the Valley Gate! The wonders of that gate will amaze you and move you onward to the goal of being totally restored to God at Christ's return.

THE VALLEY GATE

As we advance from the Old Gate to the Valley Gate, we travel through the longest wall between any two gates. This wall that originates from the Old Gate represents the place in our spiritual walk where God woos us and consistently builds our confidence in him through convincing experiences, whether large or small. Here, we also experience our "first love" for God as referenced in Revelation 2:4. You may be in this place now in your journey, or can vividly recall your time there.

At this spiritual place, we are on fire for God and passionately desire to serve and know him better. During my personal experience here, my yearning to know him better moved me to constant prayer and reading of his Word. I often looked for opportunities to share my faith with others, and if I didn't find an opportunity, I created one. When it came to church attendance, no amount of Sunday services could quench my thirst for God, so I attended every service available during the week: I went to the weekly Bible Study and mid-week prayer. In fact, I even attended praise team rehearsal when I wasn't even a member. I viewed praise team rehearsal as an opportunity to worship God, to lavish on him my adoration, praise, and love. I would sit in the back of the sanctuary and render praises to my King while the praise team rehearsed. In the event that my church didn't have a function on a particular day of the week, I would find a service at another church to attend. I just wanted to be in the presence of God and fellowship among the saints.

At home, I submerged myself in the Word, watching Christian television non-stop. I also spent enormous amounts of time on the phone, talking to friends about God and his Word. Granted, I became a bit over-zealous, so much so that some people avoided conversing with me as I tended to spiritualize EVERYTHING!

For example, one day my dad purchased a VCR at a yard sale. He inserted a video cassette to see if it worked; but the cassette got stuck. After spending 20 minutes trying to remove the video from the stubborn machine, my dad finally exploded. He angrily pounded on the VCR in hopes that the video cassette would eventually come free. It just wasn't happening. Unfortunately, this cassette happened to contain the video footage of my parents wedding. I stepped in to ease his tension and approached him the best way I knew. Tentatively, I asked my obviously agitated father a question: "Dad, do you know you can do anything in Jesus' name?"

Not a Christian at the time, my father turned in anger and yelled at me for being foolish. Then he challenged me and said mockingly, "Let me see! I'm going to sit right here on this chair and watch while you get that cassette out in Jesus' name! I've been working on that thing for a long time now. You think you're just going to show up and say, 'In Jesus' name', and that cassette will come out? C'mon, let's see it!" He sat on a nearby chair to watch me do just that. I laid my hands on the VCR and said, "In the name of Jesus, release this cassette!" I pressed eject and the video came out. My father turned pale and apologized for challenging God. I rejoiced in this great God moment. But you see, I'm trying to point out that my love and confidence in God knew no bounds at that time. Operating at an all-time high, I had silly confidence. And what's more, God was answering those "silly" prayers.

Now, I'm mature enough today to understand that those types of prayers won't always be answered. At the time, God answered my prayer in order to prove his authority to my father; he also wanted to boost my faith as I traveled along the broad wall from the Old Gate to the Valley Gate. Again, during this stage in our journey, God oftentimes answers those simple, child-like prayers to let us know he's with us and builds our confidence.

The Tower of Furnaces

But when we least expect it, an abrupt transition occurs. We go from singing and praising God to whom we constantly feel in close proximity, to feeling disconnected and distant from him. Answers to prayer suddenly disappear, with feelings of loneliness and abandonment soon taking their place.

Even at church, the joy we once felt succumbs to dryness and sorrow. At this point in our walk with God, we often become the most confused. Anguish overwhelms our spirits and our minds are inundated with unanswered questions.

Why would God shut down so abruptly, without notice or warning? We ask ourselves, "Did I sin?" "Did I blaspheme the Holy Spirit, unintentionally?" "Do I have secret sin in my heart?" "Am I not chosen?" These represent only some of the many questions we may ask ourselves during this sudden and painful transition.

Truthfully speaking, this strange silence from God signals your arrival to the Tower of Furnaces (Nehemiah 3:11), and subsequently, the Valley Gate. Here, we return again to the subject of coals, hot burning coals which heated the Tower of Furnaces!

Do you recall what Christ depicted while cooking the fish on the coals in the study of the Fish Gate? And do you recollect the symbolic purpose of the coal, when an angel took the hot ember from the Temple's altar and touched Isaiah's lips with it? It spoke of sanctification!

Well, Christ promised to clean any fish brought to him, putting them through the process of sanctification. This godly measure or practice always leads us through the burning coals of the Tower of Furnaces and the Valley Gate.

As we study this gate, you'll understand the important role this phase plays in the process of being made like Christ.

Significance of the Valley Gate

Let me provide some background on the Valley Gate to clearly grasp the spiritual meaning present there. Three main valleys surrounded the city of Jerusalem at the time of Nehemiah: Tyropoean, Kidron, and Ben Hinnom.

The Valley Gate was situated in the Tyropoean Valley. *Tyropoean* is believed to have been mistranslated by the renowned Romano-Jewish scholar, Titus Josephus, to mean "cheese makers" which, in actuality, should have been translated to "congeal." These two words are similar in the original language and essentially cheese making provides a really good description of what "congealing" means. Some dictionaries state that "congeal" means "to change from a fluid to a solid state or curdle," as the liquid state of milk changes into a solid state of cheese. Another definition of congeal is "to make rigid or fixed in ideas, principles or sentiments."

God purposed that our journey through the Valley Gate would make us firm and fixed in our Christian disposition and character, resulting in a significant change in our Christian walk. At this point, I feel it necessary to disclaim any connection between this spiritual valley and the valley of great trouble and affliction that results from sins committed or poor choices we've made. These consequences can teach us great lessons that God can use for our growth and development, once we've repented from our sins. Somehow, God in his grace manages to make even those negative consequences work together for our good and create positive outcomes from them.

However, the metaphoric valley discussed in this chapter represents the sudden trials that come as a result of living a committed, unwavering life before God. These trials typically occur without any fault of our own other than our commitment to Christ, and have no logical explanation.

Difficult challenges now beset us, with no real strategies on how to get through them. Suddenly, caught up in a whirlwind, this amazing spiritual walk takes a drastic turn, leaving us feeling confused and abandoned by our God. The by-product of these trials may cause us to temporarily struggle with sinful desires that offer to fill the void created by the valley.

The Importance of Hanun and Zanoah in the Valley

Let's take a closer look at some of the details found in the reparation of the Valley Gate.

> *The Valley Gate repaired Hanun, and the inhabitants of Zanoah; they built it, and set up the doors thereof, the locks thereof, and the bars thereof, and a thousand cubits on the wall to the Dung Gate.*

> (Nehemiah 3:13, AKJ)

First, let's focus on who Nehemiah assigned to repair this gate – Hanun and the residents of the town Zanoah. Hanun in Hebrew means "favor!" Can you believe that favor is working for you in the Valley Gate? In fact, favor with God is what causes him to bring you to this place!

Normally we hear messages that typically say the opposite – God's favor delivers us out of valleys and trials. But the Scriptures actually teach that, in certain instances, the opposite is true. Our personal development in the plan of sanctification is one of those instances when favor leads us to the valley.

The other builders were the residents of Zanoah. In this case, no specific person mentioned helped Hanun rebuild the Valley Gate, but rather, a group of people identified by the town in which they resided. Their town's name means "rejected." This meant that people from a town named "Rejection" surrounded one man named "Favor". This is one of the more difficult parts of this phase in our walk with Christ, trying to understand how we can be favored by God, yet, experiencing an immeasurable amount of rejection all around. This makes this place in our journey both, perplexing and confusing.

Thankfully, God included rejection to help you just as Zanoah helped Hanun. How exactly does this occur in the valley? We must understand the purpose for the rejection.

Often, before arriving at the Valley Gate, people express their enthusiasm and excitement over our new position in Christ's kingdom. People celebrate our passion and zeal for Christ just as they did with Jesus when he first began his ministry. Widely welcomed and celebrated, throngs of people followed him and wanted to hear his teachings. There was even a point in which the people wanted to make him King.

> *When Jesus therefore perceived that they would come and take him by force, to make him a king, he departed again into a mountain himself alone.*

> (John 6:15, AKJ)

However, it didn't take long for rejection to set in as the throngs of people began to reject his teachings; they feared the religious leaders and, in some instances, the challenges his teachings posed to their sinful nature. At one point, the large audience that once followed him soon dwindled down to the 12 disciples and a faithful few.

> *From that time many of his disciples went back, and walked no more with him. Then said Jesus unto the twelve, Will ye also go away?*

> (John 6:66-67 KJV)

In like manner, the open doors and support we experienced during our "first love" season, while journeying the Broad Wall from the Old Gate to the Valley Gate, became inaccessible at the Tower of Furnaces and the Valley Gate. Those who once celebrated and cheered our Christian development can be the same people that end up criticizing and even conspiring against us, in our Valley Gate.

Furthermore, circumstances that previously used to work out for us, no longer turn out the way we believe they would. Things begin to change. The favor we once experienced seems to vanish and our prayers are no longer answered as quickly as before. God's presence seems to be withdrawn and the joy of salvation vanishes. Here, we feel condemned, lost, and rejected by God; which is just the way God wants it because this sense of rejection helps lead us to the next section of the Valley Gate, the thousand-cubit wall.

The Vital Purpose of the 1000 Cubit Wall

Of all the other works of reconstruction and reparations found in Nehemiah 3, this is the only one that specifies the exact length of wall the builders rebuilt. It so happened that the same builders of the gate rebuilt the 1,000-cubit wall that connected it to the Dung Gate. For the sake of those wondering how much a thousand cubits equates to in United States' customary units, it translates to one thousand five hundred feet or five hundred yards – the length of five professional American football fields. It is in this wall that we find the important purpose of the Valley Gate.

In Hebrew, the symbol for the number 1,000 is an ox head. The symbol of the ox head is also the first letter of the Hebrew alphabet, *alaph*. More importantly, for our study, *alaph* also has the meaning of taming and yoking an ox and it implies to learn, and causatively, to teach. With this understanding we can safely surmise that the thousand-cubit wall signifies a place of taming and yoking an ox!

In this place God breaks, subdues, trains and domesticates, and masters the wild, powerful ox and teaches it how to obey. The wild ox symbolizes the old person in us that wars against the new, holy person the the Father declares us to be (Galatians 5:17). Again, the sanctifying work of God is the process of changing our character and nature from carnal to holy. While he declared us righteous the moment we repented and surrendered to him, sanctification ensures aligning our life and character with his declaration.

Subsequently, God brings all his children to the 1000-cubit wall to tame them. Not pretty for the ox, the taming process requires consistent beatings from a whip or a goad - to beat the stubborn nature into submission to the will of its owner. While it may seem that the owner cares little for the ox, in all actuality, the owner beats the ox out of love. It's because the owner cares greatly for the ox and has determined to own and use it, that he beats it into obedience.

In the case of Christians, it's because God favors us and has decided to own us, use us, and save us for eternity that he uses the Valley Gate to tame us. Think about it. An ox or a bull possesses enough power to utterly destroy its owner and most anything standing in its path. However, once tamed, it becomes a most docile beast, useful to yoke with another tamed ox in order to plow fields and plant seeds for harvest. If you ever have an opportunity to watch oxen plow fields, you'll notice that those once wild, powerful beasts walk straight and narrow roads while plowing! It's impressive how those beasts plow straight lines and don't swerve and waver from side to side. Although we were never more powerful than God, our sinful nature made us self-destructive and useless to God; but God helps us die to our will through rejection, suffering and fiery trials. He teaches us to walk straight and narrow paths (or a righteous walk), and walk on what the Bible calls the path with the strait (narrow) gate and narrow (difficult) road that leads to eternal life (also the path of righteousness) (Matthew 7:13-14).

Yes, the process appears harsh, but God knows that the best thing he can do for anyone he favors is to teach them to die to the flesh and live a life of obedience to Him. So, just as the Son of God "learned obedience through the things he suffered" (Hebrews 5:8), so do we.

I know it's tempting to believe and preach that those who God favors should never experience rejection and suffering, but only experience the presence of material blessings, promotions, and times of great joy. Truthfully speaking, those things alone hold no eternal value, and therefore, God does not commit to always blessing us with such things. Instead, he uses the Valley Gate and the 1000-cubit wall to equip us with an attribute that both holds eternal value and proves necessary for our Christian journey - obedience. Without obedience, we can neither follow God nor please him, let alone achieve our intended purpose by making it through the rest of the journey he has set before us as reflected in the remaining gates.

Further effects of the 1000-cubit wall

During the taming process we also become better at discerning God's voice. While undeniable, our experiences at the Old Gate didn't unquestionably mean that we learned to unmistakably hear his voice. Often, while traveling the Broad Wall, in our desire to experience God the way we did at the Old Gate, we tried to recreate similar experiences by being hyper-spiritual. Although done in good conscience, our immaturity and lack of knowledge kept us from realizing God spoke less frequent than we thought.

That explains why you'll find many babes in Christ prophesying out of emotion or proclaiming that they have a word from the Lord without scriptural basis or results to support the promised outcome. They may have good intentions, but it's not until a person gets to the Valley Gate that they begin to better understand God's voice.

At the Valley Gate, rejection and suffering develops character in us, along with the proper perspectives, sentiments, and ideas of God. The submission we learn while journeying through the 1,000-cubit wall enables us to fully embrace Paul's instructions to the Corinthian church – to be steadfast, unmovable, always abounding in the work of the Lord (1 Corinthians 15:58)!

Once we have learned obedience through suffering, we don't need God to give an explanation for anything he chooses to do or asks us to do; we simply obey. If he directs us to stop a thing, we stop. If he directs us to go or turn in a certain direction, we go or turn. If he has us just stay in place in the heat of the day, or the heat of a trial, we will stay there and not move until he gives the go-ahead. Why? We do it because rejection and suffering have helped transform our will, perspectives, ideas, and sentiments to his. Now, more mature and resilient, we can better endure through the remainder of the Christian journey that, at times, will be filled with fiery trials and persecution. Also, since we have further mortified the wild tendencies of the flesh, we are better equipped to work for the kingdom and yoke alongside another tamed Christian to plow the hard ground of the world; to prepare it for the seed of the Word, as we are now able to walk a straight and narrow road before men.

The end of the thousand-cubit wall leads us into the next phase of God's plan for us, the Dung Gate. There, we will surely put into practice the obedience learned in this phase. Let's go there to see what God has in store for us.

THE DUNG GATE

The transforming and taming journey of the Valley Gate and its thousand-cubit wall ends at the Dung Gate. The name denoting something less than desirable, indicates that this stage of our journey will most likely not be much fun. However, God, in his infinite wisdom, considers it an essential part of his plan that all Christians longing to get closer to him spend some time in this place. In fact, our obedience at the Dung Gate will determine how we advance onward, as this gate acts as a gateway to the second half of our Christian journey filled with awesome wonder. When we arrive at our spiritual Dung Gate, we show up tamed and obedient, as indicated by Rechab, the father of Malchiah, the person who rebuilt the Dung Gate in the time of Nehemiah:

> But the Dung Gate repaired Malchiah the son of Rechab, the ruler of part of Bethhaccerem; he built it, and set up the doors thereof, the locks thereof, and the bars thereof. (Nehemiah 3:14, KJV)

Rechab in Hebrew means "rider," like a person who rides a domesticated animal, such as a horse or a donkey. In this case, picture yourself as the wild, untamed ox that entered the Valley Gate, figuratively meaning, that person with untamed sinful desires still raging within them. Now, imagine being ridden out from the 1000-cubit wall by the God who tamed you there. Isn't that amazing? Normally, people don't ride oxen, except for sporting purposes; even when domesticated, their owners usually yoke them together and use them for plowing purposes. The image of God riding an ox out of the valley's 1000-cubit wall and into the Dung Gate, tells us a couple of things: one, his work to break our will and tame us was impeccable; and two, his divine work caused an animal to be used in a manner that isn't typical for it.

This image vividly highlights the work God does in any person he takes through the Valley Gate and its 1000-cubit wall: he breaks their will, brings them into total submission and obedience, and then uses them in ways quite atypical for humans to do. They carry his Name, bear his likeness and character, the message of God shining forth in their lives.

Aren't you glad he causes what is unfit to become suitable to carry him? When I think about this, I remember the Ark of the Covenant, the box in the Old Testament that represented the presence of God among Israel; Scripture tells us that God only permitted the priests to carry the ark on their shoulders once they fulfilled the requirements for sanctification. Today, God still uses the Valley Gate to sanctify our hearts. He makes us holy and worthy of his presence - fit to carry and represent him in our lives.

However, of all places to lead his children to after such a difficult and trying time at the Valley Gate, why would God lead them to a gate that in Hebrew refers to excrement, feces, or poop, as well as trash, filth, and scraping? Let's take a closer look at some important aspects of the Dung Gate from Bible times to find the answer.

Uses for the Dung Gate

Outside of this gate was the city's landfill. There, a constantly burning fire consumed the city's trash. Along with the city's trash the priests would also burn the animal dung they cleared from the Temple; dung from the animals waiting to be sacrificed. This marked the same location later known as Gehenna, which translated to the word "hell." Jesus frequently used the analogy of Gehenna, verbally painting images of the hell-fire awaiting the wicked at the end of time as -an irreversible and painful agony.

The people of that time clearly understood Christ's analogy because Gehenna was also used as a place for capital punishment. Convicted felons who warranted death were thrown into the burning fire and suffered an excruciatingly painful execution.

With this understanding, what meaning can we derive from the Dung Gate?

The Spiritual Significance of the Dung Gate

What we can gather is that this gate is the gate of personal accountability and responsibility. God brings us to the Dung Gate at this point in our spiritual walk to test the submission, integrity, and holiness that we learned and obtained at the Valley Gate and its thousand-cubit wall.

Just as the responsibility for daily removing the dung and filth from the temple belonged to the priests working there, so must we also routinely examine our lives, recognizing our bodies as the temple of God where the Holy Spirit resides (1 Corinthians 6). We need to immediately address any filth of sin that would stain and blemish us. It is at this place that we work out our "own salvation with fear and trembling" (Philippians 2:12, KJV).

Hebrews 12:1 (AJV), encourages us to "lay aside every weight, and the sin which does so easily beset us, and let us run with patience the race that is set before us."

The author of Hebrews didn't suggest that God would cast aside our sins and weights, but instead, assigned this particular task to every individual. Why? This can best be explained that by this point in our journey of sanctification, we become empowered to overcome the flesh through the obedience we learned. For such reason, James 4:7 places the responsibility on each individual to submit to God and to resist the devil and the temptation he presents, so that he would flee. Remember, God would never ask us to do anything he did not teach us and empower us to do.

I want to make clear that by no means am I suggesting that from this point forward in our walk we must begin to earn the salvation freely given to us, or that we fall back into a system of righteousness by works. Doing so would negate the work of Christ and the new covenant he established. What I am saying is that by this point in our journey, God taught us to obey at the Valley Gate, and his grace enables us to shun evil and die to the sinful desires of the flesh. I shared the following verse earlier in the book, but it's worth mentioning again. Titus 2:11-12, says:

> For the _grace_ of God that brings salvation has appeared to all men, _teaching us_ that, denying ungodliness and worldly lust, we should live soberly, righteously, and godly, in this present world;"

At the Dung Gate, we must simply reflect on our lives and conduct the grace that has influenced us and has been at work in our hearts. Here, we are no longer powerless. Those who fall into sin at this point in their walk are those who become complacent and stop taking out the waste from their temple, daily.

By not taking daily inventory of our lives, sin can go unaddressed, and little by little we can find ourselves falling into a state of compromise and sin.

Before Adam sinned in the Garden, he had to consistently choose not to eat from the Tree of the Knowledge of Good and Evil (Genesis 2:16, 17). To prove his obedience to God, Adam had to daily resist the tempting urge to eat from that tree; Eve had to do the same. Sadly, Eve became complacent and fell prey to the serpent's wiles. She sinned and Adam, unfortunately, followed her example. His transgression brought God's perfect plan to a standstill. Separation from God occurred and the law of sin and death took its reign.

In like manner, many people's journey with God comes to a halt at this gate. Like Eve, their complacency gives opportunity to the devil and their eventual return to a life of sin. We must be careful to remember that this happens to church leaders and lay people alike. No one can escape from the inevitability of falling back into sin when they stop taking daily inventory of their heart and checking sin immediately.

Scraping: the Guardian of Righteousness

As mentioned earlier, dung can be defined as "scraping," meaning "to grate harshly over a rough surface by repeated strokes of an edged instrument to create a smooth surface." This definition describes the harsh manner in which a rough surface becomes smooth by the constant strikes of an edged object. These constant strikes typify what it takes to keep our flesh in subjection to the Word of God.

This task can be very painful and, at times, grueling. Our old inner man, or flesh, wars against our new nature, the new inner man's desire to do God's will (Galatians 5:16-17). As a result, we may find ourselves torn daily between our old desires and our new desire to make holy choices. Galatians 5:24 describes it this way:

> *Now those who belong to Christ have crucified the flesh with its passions and desires.*

The Roman Empire favored the use of crucifixion as a method of execution, often nailing their prisoners to a wooden cross. A long and painful death, a successful crucifixion required edged instruments and blunt nails that were less likely to split the wood during the actual execution. The Greek meaning for crucified in this verse is "impale," and it means "to pierce with a sharp instrument."

This grueling task helps convey the seriousness with which God wants us to address and deal with the sinful desires that wage war against our new nature. He made clear that this constant scraping of sin from our lives would be painful and extremely uncomfortable, but by a commitment to live according to his Spirit and his empowering grace, God would enable us to accomplish the intended outcome. Further, the daily, yet unpleasant, priestly task of removing the dung from the Temple, exemplifies the strong commitment and devout perseverance necessary to inspect and clean our temples daily.

Faith without Works is Dead

There exists among some circles of Christianity a belief that we, as believers, do not have any work to do as it pertains to our holiness. They feel that because God has already declared us holy, his determination settles any argument to the contrary. The "Once saved, always saved" adage comes into play here, since anything that we would do to maintain holiness would make our righteousness the result of works and self-righteousness. This clearly makes evident why we must learn to correctly understand the phases, or process, of sanctification.

By the time we arrive to our Dung Gate, we have been through the sanctifying furnace of affliction at the Tower of Furnaces, the Valley Gate and the 1000-cubit wall. Our learnings at those destinations prepare us for the Dung Gate, the place where faith meets works. James 2:25 states, "Faith without works is dead." This doesn't mean that works produce faith, but faith must yield works that confirm it. In like fashion, God tests the fruit of our obedience at the Dung Gate, and sees the result of his sanctifying work.

Again, I will emphasize that we do not earn our salvation or holiness, but because they are freely given, along with the empowerment of God to learn and walk righteously, God has a right to tell us, "Go and sin no more or something worse will come upon you," (John 5:14), or "It would have been better that they had not known the way of righteousness, than to have known it and turned back to sin like a dog to its vomit," (2 Peter 2:21-22).

The Dung Gate: The Gate of Promotion

Malchiah, the builder of this gate, lent a sense of beauty to it through the meaning of his name. In the Hebrew language, the name "Malchiah" means "King appointed by Yah, or Yahweh."

We can see here that the Dung Gate is also the place where spiritual promotion occurs. It becomes very apparent that God rewards a lifestyle of constant obedience to his word and the constant denial of sinful desires. God understands the challenges we face in our struggle to choose holiness on a daily basis. However, the joy of replacing our sinful desires with his promised desire for our lives cannot be measured! And, therefore, it pleases the Lord to promote anyone who gets to this place in their journey and maintains a committed devotion to the daily task of dying to self and living uprightly.

The life of Christ beautifully illustrates the manner in which promotion at the Dung Gate takes place. On the night of his betrayal, Christ's disciple, Judas Iscariot, turned him over to the religious leaders of the time. Well aware of their plot to have him crucified, the Messiah, nonetheless, elected to spend time praying in the Garden of Gethsemane. In this documented prayer, we can see the battle between Christ's personal desires and the Heavenly Father's will. Notice the implications found in his petition.

> *Going a little farther, he threw himself down with his face to the ground and prayed, "My Father, if possible, let this cup pass from me!* <u>*Yet not what I will, but what you will.*</u>*" (Matthew 26:39)*

The cup Christ referred to was the cup of wrath that symbolized the wrath of God he would endure in his execution to pay for the sins of the world. Christ becoming the object of God's wrath would ultimately make forgiveness possible for all who repented and desired to be restored to communion with God.

In his prayer, Christ pleaded that the Father find a another means in which to make peace with his errant creation; surely there must be a better way to make the forgiveness of sin possible rather than subjecting him to a miserable death on the cross. He didn't fear the physical pain, nor did he begrudge us our salvation. The Messiah simply realized that by drinking this cup of wrath, it would result in his total separation from the Father. The fear of this estrangement caused Christ to cry out on the cross, "My God, My

God, why have you forsaken me," (Matthew 27:46b).

Here lies the miraculous dynamic in the death of Christ - how his divine nature was separated from his human nature to ensure God's plan of redemption. Yet, in order to get to that point, Christ had to forego his desire for a change of plan, and instead, chose to submit to the Father's will!

Here, we see a great moment where Christ's initial desire did not align with the Father's, and understandably so. But he laid aside his desire and asked the Father to accomplish his will, which led to his grueling execution on the Cross; as a result of his committed obedience, the Father raised him from the dead and promoted him to King of kings and Lord of lords (Revelation 19:16)!

In addition, the Father gave him a name of authority, the name above every name, and to that name, every knee will bow and confess that he is Lord, or supreme authority (Philippians 2:9-11)!

Therefore, when we find our will to be contrary to the will of God, we should pray to the Father without ceasing and yield our will in exchange for his will. This act of obedience prepares us for our spiritual promotion.

Man's Promotions

Humans have a tendency, even in churches, to promote people to positions based on talents and abilities, or status and connections. However, any spiritual promotion by man prior to our Dung Gate experience is futile, since a person has not proven the conversion of character and integrity necessary to be promoted to a consecrated position. Premature promotions often leads to people being promoted to positions they are incapable of living up to.

God only promotes those devoted to holy living, even though the process of doing so can be crushing and disheartening through the constant crucifixion of the flesh. But their character has become more Christ-like and they can be entrusted with more. While, most carnal minded people regard promotion as a means to greater status and rank; with God, it simply represents the next step up his ladder of sanctification, the Fountain Gate. Oh what a glorious experience awaits all who advance to it!

So, as a daily devotion, let us remember to do what Paul admonished the Corinthian church to do: examine and judge ourselves so that we are not judged and condemned with the world (1 Corinthians 11). That means to search our lives daily, and when we identify any waste, let us quickly address it and judge it. Let us live lives worthy of the call to holiness. Faithfully doing so will propel us to receive our spiritual promotion to the next gate in our journey, the Fountain Gate!

THE FOUNTAIN GATE

Usually between the reparation of any two gates in Nehemiah 3, a wall is mentioned. This is not the case between the Dung Gate and the Fountain Gate. Scholars believe that it's either because there was no wall there or because the wall was so short in length it wasn't worth mentioning. This is great news for anyone at the Dung Gate devoted to obedience and diligently crucifying any sinful desire that would cause them to stumble, because the proximity of these gates is a clear indication of how close we are to experiencing another great dimension in our journey of sanctification.

Nehemiah 3:15-16 gives us the names of the repairers of the Fountain Gate, who will help guide our perspective through its teaching:

> But the Gate of the Fountain repaired Shallun the son of Colhozeh, the ruler of part of Mizpah; he built it, and covered it, and set up the doors thereof, the locks thereof, and the bars thereof, and the wall of the Pool of Siloah by the King's Garden, and to the stairs that go down from the city of David. After him repaired Nehemiah the son of Azbuk, the ruler of the half part of Beth-zur, to the place over against the sepulchers of David, and to the pool that was made, and to the house of the mighty. (AKJ)

Shallun not only repaired the Fountain Gate but also the wall by the Pool of Siloah, also known as the Pool of Siloam, located in the same area near the King's Garden.

Here I wish to share some important background information about the Pool of Siloam you'll find quite significant. In the 8th century B.C., during the reign of the Judean King, Hezekiah, the King of Assyria threatened to invade Jerusalem. Although Hezekiah felt confident that the Assyrians would not be able to penetrate the great walls of the city, he did worry that the Gihon Spring's location outside its protective walls, could pose a problem as it functioned as Jerusalem's main water source. With the water source outside the city walls, even if King Hezekiah had shut the city gates and kept the Assyrian army out, the people of Judah would have still died of thirst.

To solve this dilemma, King Hezekiah came up with an innovative idea and built the very first underground aqueduct. The aqueduct connected the waters from the Gihon to the Pool of Siloah located inside the city walls by the Fountain Gate.

Here we see a divine message for God's people, even in Jerusalem's water source. It is no accident that *Gihon* in Hebrew means "paradise." As such, we could literally say that Hezekiah's innovative idea allowed water from paradise to flow into the city for everyone to drink while the gates remained shut. Stay tuned!

The Fountain Gate: The Gate of Vision

To gain a better understanding of the Fountain Gate, we must look at its meaning. The Hebrew word for fountain (ayin) means "eye," indicating that we should view the Fountain Gate as the Gate of Vision or the actual Eye Gate! Shallun's name translated in Hebrew means "requital," which means "repayment, retribution or compensation." This lends a certain significance to his position as the repairer of the Eye Gate! The name of Shallun's father, Colhozeh, in Hebrew means "every seer." Today, we refer to seers as prophets; "chozeh," the Hebrew word for "seer" means "visionary." I know that I'm giving you a lot to take in but this information profoundly impacts our understanding of this gate.

Let's take a look at Colhozeh. His name provides us insight into the purpose God gave him. Colhozeh was a seer, and while Jerusalem lay in disgrace for decades after the Judeans' release from Babylonian captivity, the meaning of his name made it highly likely that he envisioned himself and his people, once again, entering and exiting Jerusalem as a functioning city with its walls and gates fully restored. This would have meant that Jerusalem would no longer lie in ruins nor endure great trouble and disgrace. Perhaps God allowed Colhozeh, the visionary, to foresee the people of God standing strong, with liberty and freedom, worshipping the only true and living Yahweh, within a newly fortified city.

This visionary's son, Shallum, helped to do just that, by rebuilding the Fountain Gate, or Gate of Vision. His work provided recompense and payback for Colhozeh for all those sorrowful years of trouble and disgrace.

It's not farfetched to liken the Heavenly Father to Colhozeh. Despite humanity's bondage to sin, God envisioned the day when those desiring to be free from sin would see their trouble and disgrace washed away and restored back to the Father. Although it took millennia to accomplish, his son, Jesus, fulfilled that vision, and the reconciling work through Christ was the repayment to God for all the years of broken fellowship with humanity.

Why Vision becomes the Enemy's Target

Interestingly, scholars believe that this gate may have been the most devastated and damaged of all gates during the Babylonian siege because of what Nehemiah 2:13-15 states about the time Nehemiah went out to survey Jerusalem's damaged walls and gates:

And I [Nehemiah] went out by night by the Gate of The Valley, even before the dragon well, and to The Dung Port, and viewed the walls of Jerusalem, which were broken down, and the gates thereof were consumed with fire. Then I went on to The Gate of The Fountain, and to The King's Pool: but there was no place for the beast that was under me to pass. Then went I up in the night by the brook, and viewed the wall, and turned back, and entered by The Gate of The Valley, and so returned. (AKJ)

The gate underwent so much havoc that Nehemiah's mount could not get past the rubble.

In order to re-enter Jerusalem, Nehemiah had to return through the Valley Gate. This statement will prove most significant as we continue to understand the spiritual meaning of this gate.

But why would Babylon, the enemy of God's people, attack the Gate of Vision so heavily? We can best find the answer to this question by understanding why Satan attacks God's people so viciously in this phase of their Christian journey. To get to our answer, we must consider a very popular verse found in Proverbs 29:18 that reads:

> *Where there is no vision, the people perish:*
> *But he that keeps the law, happy is he. (AKJ)*

As a new Christian, I found this verse very confusing since I understood the word "perish" to mean "die." As a result, when I read this Scripture, I envisioned dead bodies lying across the streets of a city. This incorrect perspective occurred because of my lack of understanding and misinterpretation of the verse. By examining this verse through a Hebraic lens, we can gain a better understanding of the term. The Hebrew word "para" translates as "unrestrained, loosen, absolved, or set free." The NET translation of the Bible expresses the above verse as follows:

> When there is no prophetic vision
>
> The people cast off restraint,
>
> But the one who keeps the law, blessed is he!

Such simple clarity allows us to view this verse in its proper context. The Scripture actually means that where no prophetic vision exists, the people loosen in their lifestyle, or morals, and become unrestrained.

Realistically, the sad fact exists that many people's journey with God will come to a halt before ever getting to the Fountain Gate. Some say the Sinner's Prayer and ask Jesus to be the Lord of their life at the Sheep Gate but never take on the responsibility of evangelism at the Fish Gate. Others become involved with church and church functions but don't take the time to pursue an intimate relationship with God and, as a result, fail to experience the transforming wonder and power of God at the Old Gate. Typically, these carnal church folk could never testify of a true, personal, transforming encounter with God. Some get to the Valley Gate and find themselves stuck there for a long time as they struggle to fully surrender every aspect of their life in obedience to Christ.

Finally, everyone who arrives at the Dung Gate shows up fully intending to obey God and to prove their commitment to continuously take inventory of their lives; to walk in a manner pleasing to the Father. For some, the continual work of discarding the dung and trash, or simply put, mortifying the desires of the flesh, becomes too tasking; sooner or later, they become complacent, allowing secret sins to creep in little by little. Eventually, like yeast, it spreads, and hinders them from getting promoted and advancing to the Fountain Gate.

But for those who do advance to the Fountain Gate, they become a real threat to Satan and his kingdom because of the work God does in and through them from this spiritual point forward! The devil can only hope to derail those individuals' progress by having them lose sight of God's prophetic vision. Doing so will result in them losing sight of living in eternity with God, and would negatively impact their purpose of preparing a holy church for the Second Coming of Christ. The apostle Paul set his sights on Christ's return, and he encouraged Titus to do the same in Titus 2:13:

> Looking for that blessed hope, and the glorious appearing of the great God and our Savior Jesus Christ.

The enemy knows that if we lose sight of this vision, we will loosen in our lifestyle and fall back into sin, thereby halting the progress of sanctification, making us unprepared for Christ's return, and ineffective for God's use.

The "old-time" church focused on this priority of God, and constantly preached messages that compelled people to prepare themselves for Christ's return. Messages of that time constantly addressed holiness and living upright before God, and focused heavily on the return of Jesus Christ. They had people looking forward to heaven. The church of that time spoke of things holding eternal value; the atoning work of Christ on the cross, the power of his blood, baptism and communion. They also expounded on the Person of the Holy Spirit and his work of sanctification, in addition to end-time prophecy and the deliverance of God's people. Simply put, they focused on things that made salvation and living in eternity with God possible. The body of Christ, for the most part, took church, God, prayer, and personal devotion seriously. They learned the importance of addressing sin quickly. But somewhere along the line, a large part of the church lost the vision of Christ's return. As a result, a lot of the church grew complacent about the Second Coming; they put off holiness and ended up compromising their lifestyles.

In many circles of Christianity, sermons have evolved into motivational messages encouraging a humanistic and self-centered agenda. Here we see the cunning work of the devil. He knows that by getting God's people to focus on self-achievements and a comfortable lifestyle, they will soon lose their vision of Christ's return. If people can strive for and obtain satisfaction on earth, why would they yearn for heaven and focus on being ready for Jesus' return?

Sadly, the absence of God's prophetic vision leaves his people spiritually lost and disoriented. Because of this, they can sit in countless church services and walk away never understanding or knowing God better. Instead, they fully expect God to focus his attention on those things designed to make their life more comfortable and problem-free; perhaps a job promotion, a million dollar contract, fame or good health. Today, many subscribe to the belief that seeking after such things will result in a restoration of sorts. In fact, the obtainment of such things has been interpreted by many, today, to be restoration – as if these things were the most important things we lost as a result of sin, and not God himself.

The apostle Paul, however, tells us that Christians who live focused on finding total fulfillment on earth, have become enemies of the cross by default (Philippians 3:18–21).

In the third and fourth chapters of the Book of Revelation, we read of seven letters Christ wrote to the seven churches. Those seven churches represent the different sectors of the church during the end-times. Christ rebuked several of those churches. He admonished a couple of them specifically for preaching demonic doctrines that completely opposed the truth of God – one for preaching the doctrines of Jezebel, a killer of the prophets of God in the Old Testament; the other for perpetuating the demonic doctrines of the Nicolaitans, very similar to Jezebel's propaganda.

You might wonder why the church leaders failed to notice the corrupt teachings being preached from their pulpits. This can be explained by one simple fact: the loss of vision. The devil continues to accomplish the same today. He distorts Scriptures in order to introduce doctrines that appear godly, but self-gratification and anything that appeases the flesh acts as the bedrock for such heresies. Many congregations find such teachings easy to digest and embrace because they don't require self-sacrifice or a need to address sin. Sooner or later, those following such doctrines will experience spiritual derailment, potential apostasy, and the danger of not being ready at the return of Christ.

God wants his people, as a whole, to recapture the vision of Christ's Second Coming and to live an upright and holy life preparing for when the final trumpet sounds and the bridegroom returns for his bride, the church.

The Return to the Valley – a Viable Option

As an act of grace, God created a process within his plan for all who may get stuck at the Fountain Gate by losing God's vision and loosening on their lifestyle. Do you recall what Nehemiah had to do while surveying the damaged walls and gates of Jerusalem? What happened after he arrived at the Fountain Gate but failed to get through because of the vast amount of rubble? He returned back to the Valley Gate and entered Jerusalem there.

For all who lose their way at the Fountain Gate and can't get completely through it, God recycles them back to the affliction of the Valley Gate and its thousand-cubit wall. He does this to re-teach them how to see through godly lenses, adopting, once again, the sentiments and perspectives of God, thus making holiness and the Second Coming of Christ priorities. This allows the person to proceed forward to the Dung Gate to prove their obedience, again, and then onward to the Fountain Gate once more! What a painful process to start again, but what an act of grace and mercy on God's part to love us enough to try and realign us with his purpose. Now let's move forward in our learning.

Loss of Spiritual Vision Always Reflects Outwardly

Prior to death in Bible times, captors often gouged out the eyes of high ranking officials, taken as prisoners, in order to humiliate them. Samson offers an excellent example of this. Delilah, in cahoots with the Philistines, an enemy of Israel, managed to seduce Samson into sharing with her, the secret of his supernatural strength. Once she learned that cutting his long, wavy locks would strip him of his brute force, she cut his hair as soon as he fell asleep. Upon losing his strength and his ability to withstand the Philistines, they captured him and gouged out his eyes. We can clearly see what Samson could not; he failed to recognize Delilah, a Philistine woman, as the enemy because he focused more on her beauty than on his relationship with God. Simply put, he lost sight of God. This disconnect with the Lord led to his foolish disclosure of the secret to his massive strength and his inevitable inability to see at all.

The Babylonian seizure of Jerusalem, found in 2 Kings 25:1-7, provides another illustration of this particular problem. This seizure fulfilled the prophet Jeremiah's prophecy against Judah for its continual abandonment of the worship of Yahweh for the worship of false idols.

King Zedekiah, who greatly encouraged Israel's idolatry, reigned as king when God's promise of judgment came to pass and Babylon besieged the city of Jerusalem. Look at what occurred:

> *And it came to pass in the ninth year of his reign, in the tenth month, in the tenth day of the month, that Nebuchadnezzar king of Babylon came, he, and his host, against Jerusalem, and pitched against it; and they built forts against it round about. And the city was besieged unto the eleventh year of King Zedekiah. And on the ninth day of the fourth month the famine prevailed in the city, and there was no bread for the people of the land. And the city was broken up, and all the men of war fled by night by the way of the gate between two walls, which is by The King's Garden (now the Chaldeans were against the city round about:) and the king went the way toward the plain. And the army of the Chaldeans pursued after the king, and overtook him in the plains of Jericho: and all his army were scattered from him. So they took the king, and brought him up to the king of Babylon to Riblah; and they gave judgment upon him. And they slew the sons of Zedekiah before his eyes, and put out the eyes of Zedekiah, and bound him with fetters of brass, and carried him to Babylon. (AKJ)*

Notice the progression of the passage above. When the Babylonians broke through the gates of the city, Zedekiah and his army attempted to escape. They fled through the gate between two walls by the King's Garden which was the Fountain Gate, the Eye Gate, the Gate of Vision! The Babylonians pursued Zedekiah and captured him and his sons and pronounced judgment on him. First, the Babylonians killed his sons before his very *eyes,* and then, they gouged out Zedekiah's *eyes* and took him captive.

Interestingly enough, Zedekiah's experience symbolically resembles that of Samson, another biblical character who also lost sight of faithfulness and obedience to God. Both men lost their spiritual vision of leading the people in worship of Yahweh and keeping his commands. The result of losing their spiritual vision, was the loss of their physical eyesight. This same concept holds true today—a loss of spiritual vision will always reflect on our conduct and decisions and lead us to our downfall.

The Waters of Siloam

Now, let's jump ahead into the New Testament, getting a glimpse of the way Jesus used a blind man and the waters of Siloam to reverse this order in the ninth chapter of John. But let's make a quick stop in Isaiah 8:5-8 to grab hold of an important piece of information that we'll need:

> *The LORD spoke also unto me again, saying, "Forasmuch as this people refuse the waters of Shiloah that go softly, and rejoice in Rezin and Remaliah's son; Now therefore, behold, the Lord brings up upon them the waters of the river, strong and many, even the king of Assyria, and all his glory: and he will come up over all his channels, and go over all his banks: And he will pass through Judah; he will overflow and go over, he will reach even to the neck; and the stretching out of his wings will fill the breadth of your land, O Immanuel." (KJV)*

In this prophetic passage, God appeared to be enraged with the people of Judah for rejecting the gentle flowing waters of Shiloah (the same is the Pool of Siloam). Because of this rejection, he announced judgment against them. The final two words of the passage help direct us to the meaning of the water – "O Immanuel."

God only refers to one person as Immanuel, which means "God with us." Isaiah 7:14 says that the Messiah will be Immanuel, and

Matthew 1:23 finally reveals him to us - Jesus Christ! So what would the waters of Siloam have to do with the Messiah who would embody God in the flesh? Stay tuned!

Jesus at the Fountain Gate

In John chapter nine, Christ, the Messiah, unfolds the divine message of the Fountain Gate to help us understand the role it plays in our journey with God. Let's read the passage and consider the vast details:

> *Now as Jesus passed by, He saw a man who was blind from birth. And His disciples asked Him, saying, "Rabbi, who sinned, this man or his parents, that he was born blind?" Jesus answered, "Neither this man nor his parents sinned, but that the works of God should be revealed in him. I must work the works of Him who sent Me while it is day; the night is coming when no one can work. As long as I am in the world, I am the light of the world."(John 9:1-5, NKJV)*

In this instance, Jesus made it very clear that the man's blindness could not be blamed on sin, but rather that God's works might be revealed in him. Now the next two verses show us how the Fountain Gate proved relevant to this man's healing; but I want you to remember one important thing. God only promotes people to the Fountain Gate when they do not take his grace for granted at the Dung Gate, but commit themselves to its empowerment and consistently mortify the desires of the flesh. These remain poised and ready to address sin quickly, persistent in their quest to protect their holy integrity. How fitting then, that Jesus' response to his disciples' was, "Neither this man, nor his parents sinned," because the work of God that's revealed in his people at the Fountain Gate is not in response to sin.

> *When He had said these things, He spat on the ground and made clay with the saliva; and He anointed the eyes of the blind man with the clay. And He said to him, "Go, wash in the pool of Siloam" (which is translated, Sent). So he went and*

washed, and came back seeing. (John 9:6-7, NKJV)

What better place for Jesus to send this man to than to the Pool of Siloam? Do you recall the location of this pool? It was located by the Fountain Gate, the Eye Gate, the Gate of Vision. When he arrived there and washed in the gentle, flowing waters of Siloam, the blind man received his sight!

> *Therefore the neighbors and those who previously had seen that he was blind said, "Is not this he who sat and begged?" Some said, "This is he." Others said, "He is like him." He said, "I am he." Therefore they said to him, "How were your eyes opened?" He answered and said, "A Man called Jesus made clay and anointed my eyes and said to me, 'Go to the pool of Siloam and wash.' So I went and washed, and I received sight." Then they said to him, "Where is He?" He said, "I do not know." They brought him who formerly was blind to the Pharisees.(John 9:8-13, NKJV)*

Now, it's very important that we note that what happened next took place in the presence of the Pharisees, the religious leaders of the time. I like to say that what took place next took place with the church folk of that time.

> *Now it was a Sabbath when Jesus made the clay and opened his eyes. Then the Pharisees also asked him again how he had received his sight. He said to them, "He put clay on my eyes, and I washed, and I see." Therefore some of the Pharisees said, "This Man is not from God, because He does not keep the Sabbath." Others said, "How can a man who is a sinner do such signs?" And there was a division among them.*

> (John 9:14-16, NKJV)

Important Point:

> **The Fountain Gate creates division, among church folk, particularly among its church leaders.**

As we continue in our study, it will become apparent why the Fountain Gate will cause division among church folk. Let's continue.

> *They said to the blind man again, "What do you say about Him because He opened your eyes?" He said, "He is a prophet." (John 9:17, NKJV)*

Another important point to keep in mind involves this man's perception and proclamation of Christ being a <u>prophet</u>.

> *But the Jews did not believe concerning him, that he had been blind and received his sight, until they called the parents of him who had received his sight. And they asked them, saying, "Is this your son, who you say was born blind? How then does he now see?" His parents answered them and said, "We know that this is our son, and that he was born blind; but by what means he now sees we do not know, or who opened his eyes we do not know. He is of age; ask him. He will speak for himself." His parents said these things because they feared the Jews, for the Jews had agreed already that if anyone confessed that He was Christ, he would be put out of the synagogue. Therefore his parents said, "He is of age; ask him."*
>
> (John 9:18-23, NKJV)

Sadly, instead of rejoicing with him over this miracle, the blind man's parents preferred to disassociate themselves from the matter; deflecting and deferring all questions and pressure to their son for fear of being put out of the synagogue.

This happened because the Fountain Gate divides those who prefer associations, affiliations, or positions from those who hunger for truth.

> *So they again called the man who was blind, and said to him, "Give God the glory! We know that this Man [Jesus] is a sinner." He answered and said, "Whether He is a sinner or not I*

do not know. One thing I know: that though I was blind, now I see." Then they said to him again, "What did He do to you? How did He open your eyes?" He answered them, "I told you already, and you did not listen. Why do you want to hear it again? Do you also want to become His disciples?" Then they reviled him and said, "You are His disciple, but we are Moses' disciples. We know that God spoke to Moses; as for this fellow, we do not know where He is from." The man answered and said to them, "Why, this is a marvelous thing, that you do not know where He is from; yet He has opened my eyes! Now we know that God does not hear sinners; but if anyone is a worshiper of God and does His will, He hears him. Since the world began it has been unheard of that anyone opened the eyes of one who was born blind. If this Man were not from God, He could do nothing." They answered and said to him, "You were completely born in sins, and are you teaching us?" And they cast him out. (John 9:24-34, NKJV)

After the man challenged the church leaders with truth, they put him out of the church. They put more weight on their perceived association with Moses than the facts that lay before them. More importantly, because they thought so highly of themselves, they became corrupt and manipulated God's Law for self-gain. On this occasion, they looked for a way to discredit the amazing work Christ had done in this man, as it went against the belief system they burdened and manipulated people with.

Before we continue reading the remainder of the passage in John 9, let's pay a visit to the book of Job, as his experience will help us more fully understand the remainder of the Fountain Gate and the effect it has on our lives.

The Often Overlooked Outcome with Job

For those who may not be familiar with Job in the Old Testament, the Bible describes him as "...pure and upright, one who feared God and turned away from evil," (Job 1:1). He was the wealthiest

man in his region and a very fruitful one, at that. Job boasted a total of 10 children, 7 sons and 3 daughters. His children were really
close knit and loved to party. A popular custom among his sons
entailed taking turns hosting huge celebrations in their homes;
apparently, they would eat and drink the night away (Job 1:4).
However, Job's greatest concern was that neither he nor his children sin against God. This burden grew to such an extent, that on
the day following their feasts, he would pray for their sanctification and offer sacrifices to God for fear that "perhaps my children
have sinned and cursed God in their hearts" (Job 1:5).

This verse demonstrates Job's commitment to ensuring that he
and his children remained righteous before God – he offered
sacrifices on the possibility that they may have sinned before the
Lord. Well, the time came when Job's life went haywire, his greatest fears finally coming to pass.

Through a series of robberies and natural disasters, he lost all his
wealth and, more importantly, his children (Job 1:13-19). Job
grieved in despair, but even then, took great pains "not to sin by
blaming God," (Job 1:22, NLT), and made one of his most renowned statements:

> He said, "Naked I came from my mother's womb, and naked
> I will return there. The LORD gives, and the LORD takes
> away. May the name of the LORD be blessed!"

> *(Job 1:21)*

To bless God after such a tragedy should certainly be commended,
but not too much time passed before Job changed his tune. What
provoked his change in demeanor may surprise you. We can thank
three of Job's friends, Eliphaz, Bildad, and Zophar, for the change
in Job's attitude. Rather than offering him words of comfort and
compassion, they began to accuse him of sinning against God,
and tried persuading him to repent (Job 4-27). They perceived
such calamities as a punishment from God, reserved only for the

wicked; this could never happen to a truly righteous man!

The way these three men so eloquently spoke of God made their discourse seem very compelling. Upon further inspection, it appears that these men could only offer surface knowledge of all God's attributes that they claimed to know so well.

Several Scriptures seem to infer that Job and his pals actually subscribed to similar doctrines before Job's hardship. In Job's lengthy responses to the other's allegations, we'll find indications that Job also shared their belief that only sinners suffered; they also believed that God blessed the righteous man and protected him from harm. His calamities, however, created a dichotomy between his beliefs and his reality. The great polarity between the two confused Job causing him to grow weary and angry with God. He blamed his Creator for his hardships, questioning how God allowed bad things to happen to good people.

This poor man experienced feelings of betrayal, believing God failed to protect him from all of these hardships. He even accused God of not living up to his own standards. With Job in a confused state of despair, God eventually stepped in to address his complaints. He presented him with a series of questions that challenged Job's knowledge, understanding and perspective of God. With each question God asked, Job realized more and more his own insignificance plus his giant-sized inability to truly know and understand the all-knowing, sovereign God. Aware that he had conducted himself foolishly because of his skewed perspective of God, His character, attributes, and ways, Job confessed the following, greatly revelatory, statement in Job 42:1-6:

> *Then Job answered the LORD and said: "I know that you can do everything. And that no purpose of yours can be withheld from you. You [God] asked, 'Who is this [referring to Job] who hides counsel without knowledge?' Therefore I have uttered what I did not understand, Things too wonderful for me, which I did not know. Listen, please, and let me speak;*

you said, 'I will question you, and you shall answer me.' "I have heard of you by the hearing of the ear, but now my eye sees you. Therefore I abhor myself, And repent in dust and ashes." (NKJV)

Notice the statement in verse 5, where Job provides us with great revelation. "Shama," the Hebrew word for "heard," means to "hear intelligently." On the other hand, the Hebrew word, "shema," for the word "hearing," can be defined as something heard; "to hear a report, rumor, sound, or announcement."

"Rumors" are synonymous with words like hearsay, speculation, and gossip. While not all rumors are false, the word is typically associated with misinformation, or simply false information, and disinformation, meaning, information that is deliberately false. In the context of Job's statement, that is exactly how he uses "rumors." He was declaring, "I had been serving you based on rumors, but now, my Fountain Gate, my Eye Gate, has been opened and I can clearly see you!"

He realized that his perspective of God had been formed by false information. Upon coming to this realization at the end of his great trial, he made the liberating statement, "but now my eye sees you!" In essence, Job was saying, "The beliefs I held, among others, that bad things could never happen to righteous people and that all hardships were punishments sent from God, were nothing but rumors based on false information that shaped my image of you. Today, God, those rumors and inaccurate beliefs have been wiped away and I clearly see who you really are!"

In like manner, the Pharisees, in John 9, also subscribed to a belief system formed by rumors. When they threw the man healed from blindness out of the synagogue, they acted out of the erroneous conviction that no one should be healed on the Sabbath. Such a command cannot be found in Scripture; instead, it was a rumor created from misinformation, or misleading information. When the healed man questioned their rumors, they became enraged, and expelled the man from their synagogue.

Back to the Healed Blind Man

Let's see what occurred in John 9:35-38 when Jesus learned that the man had been thrust from the church.

> *Jesus heard that they had thrown him out, so he found the man and said to him, "Do you believe in the Son of Man [a reference to the Messiah]?" The man replied, "And who is he, sir, that I may believe in him?" Jesus told him, "**You have seen him**; he is the one speaking with you." He said, "Lord, I believe," and he worshiped him.*

To obtain his physical healing, the man washed his eyes with the waters of Siloam that came from the Gihon Spring (which, again, means "Paradise"), as Christ commanded; as a result, he perceived Christ to be a prophet. However, when when Jesus opened his spiritual eyes in their second encounter, the Lord enabled the man to recognize Christ not only as a prophet but, more importantly, as the actual Messiah and Lord! This revelation came about because he washed, not in natural water, but in who Isaiah had referred to as the "gentle flowing waters of Siloam" (Isaiah 8:6), the Living Water come down from Paradise – O, Immanuel – Jesus Christ! At this revelation, the man bowed down and worshipped Him.

The Pharisees, however, continuously rejected God's offer to wash in the "gentle flowing waters of Siloam" as Isaiah prophesied (Isaiah 8:6), and by it, failed to receive spiritual sight; they made themselves the subjects of God's wrath. Because they remained spiritually blind, they continued to live by and teach rumors about God that kept people from the true knowledge of him. Instead, they became, as Christ put it, the blind leading the blind (Matthew 15:14; Luke 6:39).

The Purpose of the Fountain Gate in Our Lives

Our time at the Fountain Gate helps rid us of all rumors about God that could be leveraged by the enemy. Satan wants to "steal, kill, and destroy" our true vision, or true understanding of God, and derail us from our Christian journey. As with Job, our adversary will attempt to take areas where we have misconceptions of God to antagonize us and provoke anger and resentment in us towards God. If he proves to be unsuccessful in accomplishing that, he will use the misconceptions and erroneous outlooks of church leaders to challenge our true understanding of God. Just like the blind man, we also could very well be ostracized, rejected, and mistreated by church folk, all in the name of God.

On one particular occasion, while conducting a conference based on the material included in this book, a woman approached me with tears in her eyes and shook my hand tightly. With a trembling voice, she said, "Today, you have answered a question that I've had for seven years." I wondered what Bible question I had answered through the course of the teachings that would affect her so strongly. As I went to release her hand, she squeezed it tighter and said, "Seven years ago, my daughter died." At that moment, my heart sank. With her eyes fixed on mine, she went on to say, "A year later, my husband died." At that point, I practically started crying myself just to think of the heartache and sorrow she had endured. She proceeded to say, "I was told that my daughter died because I didn't have enough faith for her healing." She squeezed my hand even tighter and her lip began to tremble as she asked me, "What mother wouldn't believe God hard enough for him to heal her daughter?" About to interject something, she spoke over me and said, "Then I was told that my daughter died because she had a generational curse!" And then, in an instant, she smiled and uttered the most incredibly liberating words, "But today, I realize, it was just a rumor!" Freed from seven years of bondage instigated by rumors about God, this woman testified that before her daughter died she spent a great deal of time working in ministry. However, since her daughter's death, this woman's anger with God kept her at odds with him because her lack of a true knowledge of God led her to believe that he had failed her. But, as she rejoiced in the liberty from her new understanding of the Word of God, she said, "Now, I will be like that ox [at the Valley Gate's thousand-cubit wall] steadfast, unmovable, always abounding in the work of the Lord!" And she went back into working in ministry, right where she belonged.

Thank God that through his grace and plan of sanctification, he leads us to this gate, knowing that, like Job, we can be righteous but misguided and in need of clarity. Sometimes we still need the occasional tweaking to clear our vision. While God certainly promoted us to the Fountain Gate because of our determination to resist sin, we, as in the case of Job, may develop erroneous perspectives of God based on inaccurate teachings, but these false rumors need to be addressed before we can proceed any further. Satan's goal to disrupt our walk with God via false rumors, rob us of our vision and goal of striving for the mark of the high calling and preparing to meet our Messiah at his Second Coming. This causes us to make compromises that loosen our convictions — Satan realizes this is his only hope of getting a person committed to holiness at the Dung Gate to fall back into sin and derail them.

But similar to the blind man in John 9, when God brings us to this gate, he reveals his work in us as he washes us in the gentle, flowing water of Siloam – Jesus! Here, he redirects our mind to the most important aspect we must remember of him—not just a performer of miracles, not just a prophet, as the blind man had concluded after his healing, but as the Messiah – the Savior.

Today, preachers present Jesus as a way-maker, as someone who can regularly meet our needs. They boast of how he can fulfill our dreams, restore our self-esteem, bear our burdens and be our friend and brother. While all of these hold true, we hear less and less of him as Messiah. And here, we regain that perspective in our journey and obtain a renewed passion for salvation.

Here, as mentioned previously, God dispels the rumors that would cause us to loosen in our walk. I must warn you, however, that banishing rumors from our lives comes at the cost of associations, relationships, and even status; you will experience pushback, criticism, and insults from those still being led by dangerous rumors. At times, they may even use intimidation tactics to try to degrade, belittle, discourage and discount those with clear perspectives that line up with God's truth, even to the point of having their followers disassociate themselves from you. But the sacrifice is well worth it. Remain faithful and focused because if you can get through this phase of your journey successfully, you'll begin to bear fruit in the King's Garden by your Fountain Gate, as the Bible indicates; you will leave the valley and advance upward to the Water Gate – the gate of spiritual elevation.

THE WATER GATE

And the temple servants who were living on Ophel worked up to the area opposite the Water Gate toward the east and the protruding tower. (Nehemiah 3:26)

While every gate up to this point experienced some rebuilding or repairing, the verse above makes no mention of reparations being done to the Water Gate. The only work that occurred happened in an area opposite the gate. As a result, many scholars strongly believe that the Water Gate never suffered any damage during the Babylonian invasion. Later, we will understand why this would have been the case.

Here, we need to further investigate the importance of the Water Gate's location. Positioned on the east side of Jerusalem, those journeying through this gate in the order described in Nehemiah 3, discover something significant. The Water Gate leads us closer to the East Gate due to the close proximity between the two gates. What makes this so important?

When we study the Bible closely, particularly, end-time prophecy, we learn that east, prophetically, signifies deliverance.

Throughout Scripture, the revelation of all prophecies and spiritual symbolism regarding the east, point us to the ultimate deliverance of God's people at Christ's Second Coming. And by ultimate deliverance, I'm referring to mankind's redemption from this fallen earth, which will be the subject of God's final act of wrath.

In fact, the deliverance of God's people from earth is the exact subject matter of the East Gate. Therefore, the Water Gate plays a pivotal role in preparing us for the Second Coming of Jesus Christ.

The Significance of the Water Gate

So what significance does this Water Gate hold in our Christian journey? The following Scripture will help us understand:

> *They went over the Fountain Gate and continued directly up the steps of the City of David on the ascent to the wall. They passed the house of David and continued on to the Water Gate toward the east.*

(Nehemiah 12:37)

To advance from the Fountain Gate to the Water Gate, people had to walk up the steps of the city of Jerusalem that could be found on a wall known as the "ascent wall." By virtue of those steps, people arrived at an elevated place where the Water Gate was situated.

Here, at this gate, God grants us insight into the true definition of spiritual elevation. Many sectors of Christianity frequently offer varying definitions for this particular term:

1. A place in God, where we regularly witness our spiritual gifts at work or observe signs and wonders operating at a greater degree than usual in our lives.

2. A promotion within the ministry.

3. An increase in favor that results in the expansion of our ministries or an upsurge in our finances and personal business endeavors.

For this reason, we must earnestly strive to understand its meaning in the context of the journey God laid out for us in the message of Jerusalem's gates. While some of the things mentioned may at times be a byproduct of spiritual elevation, one should not assume that these will always occur or that these represent God's ultimate purposes for bringing us to "elevation."

The ultimate, eternal purpose of God for leading his people to higher, spiritual ground far exceeds temporal reasons that will vanish with time and life's changing seasons.

To better understand God's intentions for elevation, we must keep in mind what transpired at the gate leading up to the Water Gate.

It was at the Fountain Gate where many of us found ourselves like Job, righteous, but with a skewed outlook on God, or at least a limited one, due to erroneous doctrines and teachings we may have learned and followed. The experience of that gate emptied us of the many misconceptions those doctrines and teachings formed in us of both God and Scripture. And while those misconceptions resulted from either innocent misinterpretation of Scripture, or maliciously construed teachings by individuals who we believed in, either way, Satan's intent with such error was to take our focus and vision from the true knowledge of God, derail us from our walk of salvation, make ineffective our witness for God, and to prevent us from preparing for Christ's Second Coming.

So, upon our arrival at the place of the Water Gate, he birthed in us a desperate hunger to know him better via the unadulterated Word of God.

The Effects of True Spiritual Elevation

The Israelites displayed that hunger when they arrived at this elevated place in Nehemiah 8. Once the walls and gates of Jerusalem had been rebuilt and repaired, the people gathered together before the Water Gate, eager to know the true God and the Book of the Law (God's holy book at the time).

Let's take a look at what transpired in the lives of God's people when they gathered at the Water Gate, as it set precedence to what occurs in our lives when we experience spiritual elevation:

And all the people gathered themselves together as one man in the street that was before the Water Gate; and they spoke to Ezra the scribe to bring the book of the Law of Moses, which the LORD had commanded to Israel.

So Ezra the priest brought the law before the assembly which included men and women and all those able to understand what they heard. This happened on the first day of the seventh month.) So he read it before the plaza in front of the Water Gate from dawn till noon before the men and women and those children who could understand. All the people were eager to hear the book of the law. (Nehemiah 8:1-3)

Ezra the scribe stood on a towering wooden platform constructed for this purpose. Standing near him on his right were Mattithiah, Shema, Anaiah, Uriah, Hilkiah, and Maaseiah. On his left were Pedaiah, Mishael, Malkijah, Hashum, Hashbaddanah, Zechariah, and Meshullam. Ezra opened the book in plain view of all the people, for he was elevated above all the people. When he opened the book, all the people stood up. Ezra blessed the LORD, the great God, and all the people replied "Amen! Amen!" as they lifted their hands. Then they bowed down and worshiped the LORD with their faces to the ground. (Nehemiah 8:4-6)

Jeshua, Bani, Sherebiah, Jamin, Akkub, Shabbethai, Hodijah, Maaseiah, Kelita, Azariah, Jozabad, Hanan, Pelaiah—all of whom were Levites—were teaching the people the law, as the people remained standing. They read from the book of God's law, explaining it and imparting insight. Thus the people gained understanding from what was read. Then Nehemiah the governor, Ezra the priestly scribe, and the Levites who were imparting understanding to the people said to all of them, "This day is holy to the Lord your God. Do not mourn or weep." For all the people had been weeping when they heard the words of the law. (Nehemiah 8:7-9)

Upon their arrival at the Water Gate, the Israelites were hungry to hear and learn about God by virtue of the Book of the Law. Up unto that point, this generation only had a limited experience of God. Their recent trouble and disgrace as a people had humbled them, and God's grace displayed to them through the rebuilding of the walls and gates produced an open-hearted eagerness to truly know their God according to Scripture.

Their eagerness to know the Divine One who had so graciously rebuilt and repaired their city walls and gates, warranted a response from God. He responded by giving them the characteristics that made it conducive for him to reveal himself to them corporately – and only God can provide those attributes and only to those who genuinely hunger for it. Those attributes, according to Nehemiah 8, included: divine unity; a hunger and eagerness to know God through the written words of the Book of the Law; a divine ability to understand their true meaning; and for those who were teachers, an ability to communicate the proper meaning of those Scriptures and an ability to cause the people of God to understand them. Let's discuss these attributes in more depth as they relate to spiritual elevation.

Divine Unity

The first notable attribute was a divine unity experienced by the community of people at the Water Gate. Please note that in the journey of the Christian life, divine unity organically occurs at the Water Gate, or during spiritual elevation; it accomplishes one of God's objectives in his people at this gate. True unity helps us identify those of the community who dwell on a higher spiritual ground. In a moment, we will see how that type of oneness came about in Nehemiah's time and how God can make that oneness possible today.

Many church leaders have committed to praying for such unity to occur. Many feel discouraged when they see little progress made. In many cases, we may actually see the opposite when individuals in the church and church groups look to achieve their own interest.

When we make God and the church experience a means to fulfilling self-serving agendas, some of the results will include: self-exaltation and aggrandizement, competition in various forms, quarrels over titles and positions, and an unhealthy, ambitious drive for notoriety and fame.

Furthermore, our churches are turned into franchises competing for patrons and members instead of working together, being kingdom-minded, and winning souls for Christ. Godless cliques may be formed, often under the guise of "fellowships," that cause discord among God's people. The love of money seeps in, and generating more of it becomes the mission and focus. Church leaders may become like kings dominating the lives of many Christians. Pleasing, exalting, promoting, and providing a lavish lifestyle for the leader becomes the purpose. Our "gospel" becomes humanistic, easy on sin and light on spiritual matters; heavy on achieving our personal goals and satisfying fleshly desires. All these results, the product of lost spiritual vision and being carnal-minded, prevent divine unity from occurring.

Doctrinal differences over biblical matters, often irrelevant for salvation, also hinder divine unity from occurring among the body of Christ. We witnessed an example of this in the account between the healed blind man and the Pharisees in the previous chapter.

I remember an occasion when I received an invitation to speak at a church. After I accepted the invitation, an elder from the church called me and questioned me on my beliefs. I didn't mind him doing his due diligence, after all, he really didn't know me that well.

We agreed on all the major points of Christianity, but we reached an impasse over a minor issue where we could no longer see eye to eye. Determined to prove me wrong, he began to raise his voice. Insisting that I knew nothing about the subject, he proceeded to recite several Bible verses to me and wouldn't allow me to speak. Refusing to hear me out, he cut me off and finally rescinded my invitation to speak.

I was completely open to having a discussion with him about the area of doctrine we didn't agree on. However, a constructive conversation was not an option for him, or even agreeing to disagree being that it wasn't a major doctrinal point.

To make matters worse, after this unpleasant encounter, I came across the two ladies from his church, who initially recommended me as a speaker. They obviously felt awkward, only speaking to me briefly before hurrying along their way. Now, this situation did little to glorify God and certainly failed to make unity, even remotely, possible.

Obviously, immaturity played a vital part in the above example, a common obstacle to maintaining harmony in the body. As most Christians operate at different levels of experience and maturity, these varying stages can result in fractured relationships and incorrect assessments that make it difficult for people to meet others at the level they're at.

For example, people at the "Old Gate" phase of their journey may presume, like Job's friends, that those struggling at the Valley Gate have a sin problem. Their immaturity and lack of understanding about this particular experience prevent them from seeing God's will in action. The same situation applies to those saved by grace at the Sheep Gate. Convinced that those at the Dung Gate strive to obtain salvation through works, they fail to see how faith is proved by works, an essential process of Christian growth.

However, at the elevated place of the Water Gate, we possess a spiritual perspective that enables us to recognize the deterrents to spiritual unity which include sin, error and immaturity. Those of us who successfully make it to this elevated state, do so by learning to put away such hindrances, since these impediments cannot pass through this gate. Why? Upon arriving at the Water Gate, God has used the previous gates to prepare us for higher ground. At the Fountain Gate, right before the Water Gate, humility sets in when we learned, like Job and the blind man that was healed, that there were serious gaps in our knowledge and understanding of God and his Word.

Yes, we may have experienced different aspects of him along the different phases of our journey, but this gate helped us to recognize the erroneous beliefs we had adopted along the way, blinding us to the complete truth.

Thus, the Fountain Gate acted as the catalyst to creating a God-designed void that developed into an insatiable hunger to truly know him and his Holy Scriptures. This pressing desire becomes the common denominator shared among all who arrive at the Water Gate, the root cause for the unity found there. Satisfying our need for the true God is all that matters there. And we, in true elevation, first turn to his written Word to satisfy this need!

True Spiritual Elevation Creates a Hunger for Scripture

Now, this may be a pivot for many who measure elevation by the amount of prophesies, dreams and visions they claim to have; possibly a preacher telling them they are going to be taken to another level or dimension in God. And while prophesies, dreams, and visions have their place in kingdom theology, many, wrongfully, consider them to be the end-all-be-all when it comes to God and ministry.

But our minds and understanding become elevated at the Water Gate once we realize that his Word reigns *above* anything else.

In their hunger to know God, the people in Nehemiah 8 asked Ezra, the priest, to bring out the Book of the Law; and when he did, they listened to its reading for at least six hours. No one complained about having to listen to these Scriptures for such a length of time. Instead, God gave them the ability to truly comprehend what the priests were reading.

That meant that God allowed them to capture the spirit and

meaning of the Scriptures they read to them, compelling them to want to hear more.

Any moment when God enables a person to understand the true spirit and meaning of Scripture, that Scripture becomes what the Greeks refer to as *rhema*. *Rhema* refers to the living voice of God; and when the Scriptures become *rhema* to you, it means that God allowed you to hear his living voice in them.

To put it plainly, *rhema* represents the divine moment when God, the true author of the Scriptures, supernaturally enables you to understand his original intent, purpose, and meaning of Scripture.

Furthermore, when prophecies and biblical symbolism become *rhema*, God allows you to understand the true fulfillment of those prophecies – we won't have to keep guessing and taking stabs at it once we hear the living voice of God.

During his ministry, Christ often used the phrase, "He that has an ear to hear, let him hear." Often, Christ used the natural ear as a metaphor to make the listener aware that there was a deeper and spiritual meaning to what preceded that phrase; yet only God could open the spiritual "ear" to discern its meaning.

Case in point, when Christ taught the crowds about the kingdom of God, oftentimes he used parables, aka, stories orchestrated to help convey spiritual or moral lessons. On each occasion, Pharisees generally resisted the teachings of Christ, refusing to accept him as their Messiah. These corrupt teachers of the law found themselves incapable of comprehending the messages contained in his parables.

After telling the Parable of the Sower (Matthew 13), Christ took his disciples aside to explain its meaning "…because it was given unto [them] to know the mysteries of the kingdom of heaven, but to [the Pharisees] it [was] not given," (Matthew 13:11).

The disciples had proven their sincere desire to follow and know God and his Son. Only those who approach God in such a manner will truly experience the rhema of his Word; to others it remains a mystery.

This explains why those unwilling to be transformed by God, read the Bible with skepticism. They do not catch its meaning, oftentimes labeling it as confusing, out-dated, and out of touch with modern society. They frequently misinterpret and misapply the Word of God.

But the tell-tell signs of an encounter with the rhema Word of God include a repentant heart, and an overwhelming sense of gratitude. Empowered by this experience, they bear the true fruit of God.

The community at the Water Gate, in Nehemiah 8, displayed the characteristics of a repentant heart after mourning and weeping upon hearing the words of the law; the people proved that they did, indeed, have "ears to hear," capturing God's heart in them.

In like manner, before arriving at the Water Gate, we heard and read Scriptures and often gave them meaning based on our immature and limited understanding or according to the beliefs of the Christian leaders who influenced us. But at the place of elevation, God enables us to capture the spirit and comprehend the meaning of the words written for us in his holy book; by opening our spiritual ears, he allows us to discern the *rhema*, or *living voice*, within them.

While some may have experienced moments when the Word of God became rhema for them, those moments can in no way be compared to the depth of revelation that only occurs at the Water Gate!

True Elevation Enables Teachers to Communicate Rhema

Those receiving the rhema of God's Word in Nehemiah 8, grasped God's true intentions, motives, determinations, desires, and purpose in the fullness of what they heard read to them. The outcome was, they understood and knew God better.

Interestingly, this ability to understand the meaning of the law extended beyond those listening at the elevated place; those reading the Word could rightly explain and interpret them as well! They did not take verses out of context, nor pull one word out of a verse and fashion a self-serving message from it. No! They communicated the true meaning of God's Word and revealed the heart of God in the passages they explained. We still need this type of preaching today.

Often times, preachers base their messages heavily on their present gate experience or on other gates previously visited. For example, preachers still at the "Old Gate" will focus their messages heavily on signs and wonders or encounters with God. Those who have made it up to the "Valley Gate" preach mostly about deliverance from trials and tribulations and coming out of dry seasons, but not much else.

While we appreciate these sermons shared at their appropriate times, we need to hear messages birthed from a place of true spiritual elevation. We require the rhema, the living voice of God, found within each gated phase of our spiritual voyage; ones that relay the intention and purpose of God as it relates to the gospel of Jesus Christ, the sanctifying work of his Spirit, and preparation for his Second Coming.

Without this understanding, sermons will lack the substance to equip Christians for the work of ministry and the building up of the church. It will prevent the church from maturing and measuring up to the full and complete standard of Christ (Ephesians 4:12-13).

But when we understand the overall message, true meaning, intentions, and purposes of God's Word as a whole, and fit each stage of our journey into the whole of it, it becomes what Paul refers to in 2 Timothy 2:15, as the rightly divided word of truth (the message of truth taught accurately) and the water Christ uses to wash and sanctify his church (Ephesians 5:25b-27).

It is the word of truth, accurately taught, that is spirit and life (John 6:63) - living, active and sharper than any two-edged sword (Hebrews 4:12).

In fact, only the accurate dissertation of the word of God can generate faith in the hearts of those who listen. Romans 10:17 says, "So then faith comes by hearing, and hearing by the word of God." Guess what Greek word for hearing is used in this verse? The word rhema, of course! A word, not perceiving sound with the natural ear, but discerning the voice of the living Yahweh!

Faith can be produced in the hearts of listeners only when we effectively communicate God's true intentions, ideas, perspectives, and determinations in the spoken Word of God. Roman's 10:14-15 explains it this way:

> *How then will they call on him in whom they have not believed? And how will they believe in him of whom they have not heard? And how will they hear without a preacher? And how will they preach, except they be sent? As it is written, how beautiful are the feet of them that preach the gospel of peace, and bring glad tidings of good things! (AKJ)*

This means that, in many cases, faith relies heavily on the mercy of God's Word being communicated in truth and accuracy; and God intends that his preachers be able to do exactly that.

Again, we are not talking about the ability to put a good sermon together to motivate the crowds, but the accurate explanation of the Word of God. Once accomplished, salvation becomes available and the people learn to experience first-hand, Christ's words, "And you shall know the truth, and the truth shall make you free" (John 8:32).

Satan's Only Option with Truth

For this reason, Satan endeavors so hard to keep us from true spiritual elevation, because there God's Word becomes *rhema* to us. We become empowered with the most effective and devastating weapon against Satan and the kingdom of darkness, the rightly divided word of truth which produces conviction, repentance, faith, freedom from sin, and sanctification!

Satan's prior relationship with the Almighty means that he retains some understanding of Scripture; he knows that "Heaven and earth will pass away, but [God's] words will never pass away," (Luke 21:33), and that "The grass withers, the flower fades: but the word of our God shall stand forever," (Isaiah 40:8). Since he's very aware of the power inherent in God's Word, the only option left to him requires that he blind people to such truths. More often than not, he fabricates rumors filled with distorted Bible verses to deceive the listener and make the Word of no effect.

If you recall, Satan used Scriptures when tempting Jesus, but he spoke these words outside the spirit and meaning of what God intended, thus becoming powerless words (Matthew 4:1-11).

Christ responded to Satan with the rhema word, empowered with spirit and life. Spoken from the source, Christ's words were expressed with accuracy, and thus, effective – and Satan had to flee!

Therefore, ministers of the Gospel, must speak from this Water Gate. Messages preached from here embody the precise and true Word of God. Filled with his original intentions, his desires, perspectives, and will, these words will stand forever!

That is why, despite Babylonian invasion, the Water Gate stood, because it represented the true Word of God!

In True Elevation, the Scriptures Become Supreme Authority

Now take notice what else happened at the Water Gate:

> *Ezra the scribe stood on a towering wooden platform con-*
> *structed for this purpose…Ezra opened the book in plain view*
> *of all the people, for he was elevated above all the people. When*
> *he opened the book, all the people stood up. (Nehemiah 8:4-5)*

At the Water Gate, the people also developed and displayed a new level of respect and honor for God's word. Their newly found reverence for the Scriptures moved them to position the opened Book above them on an elevated platform. A greatly symbolic moment for them, it indicated their willful subjection to it.

Before experiencing true, spiritual elevation, many Christians fail to fully submit to the absolute authority of Scripture. Some center their loyalties on the outlooks of denominational teachings and church leaders even when their teachings do not align with the full truth of the Word of God. Yet, their inadequate knowledge of the truth move them to regard those erroneous teachings as the supreme authority and standard for their lives.

One instance of incomplete knowledge lies in the subject of the Holy Spirit. I wholly believe in following the leading of the Spirit but also realize that people often get confused due to preconceived ideas about how it all works. Case in point: I used to place more weight on my feelings and emotions than on the Word of God. I had created a "voice of God," or a "feeling" that I interpreted as the leading of the Holy Spirit, and strictly lived by it. So many times, I wouldn't do something unless I felt "the spirit" lead me, even when the Word of God granted me full permission.

Often, I used to pray for people and my "holy spirit" would give them Scriptural sounding words of wisdom and knowledge for them, but time and evidence proved those prophecies incorrect. That same fabricated "holy spirit" led me to perform a lot of tasks that appeared spiritual in nature, but when I matured, I learned that they lacked the substance of God. I relied on this "voice" to guide me throughout my day, letting it influence vital choices and decisions in life. I certainly gave it more weight than the written Scriptures.

And, like me, many believers, in their zeal to hear from God and be led by him, have unwittingly participated in this type of error; turning to this self-generated "leading of the Holy Spirit," they continuously yield to it as their supreme authority and power. Such things make us live with the Book *closed* as we don't regard the Scriptures as highly as they ought to be.

Other people simply live according to their flesh and refuse to subject their lives to the full counsel of the Word; they pick and choose only portions of Scripture they feel comfortable following and reject the rest.

But those at the Water Gate no longer feel satisfied being led by their feelings and emotions. Casting rebellion aside, we seek a true, undefiled understanding of the Word of God and a desire to follow it unequivocally -- that's exactly what we get in the place of elevation! At this Gate, we wholeheartedly understand the veracity of the written Word of God. We submit ourselves to it, and place it above our lives as our supreme authority. It becomes the constitution that rules and directs our lives and holds us accountable. We discover in this place that we can finally comprehend what the Psalmist meant when he said, "Your word is a lamp unto my feet, and a light unto my path" (Psalm 119:105)!

Spiritual Elevation Creates a Greater Level of Worship

Ezra blessed the LORD, the great God, and all the people replied "Amen! Amen!" as they lifted their hands. Then they bowed down and worshiped the LORD with their faces to the ground. (Nehemiah 8:6)

Once a proper understanding of the Word of God is produced in the lives of those who experience elevation, an elevated outlook of God results, and subsequently, an elevated level of worship, as well.

Notice in the verse above when it reads, "Ezra blessed the LORD," it paused to add, "the great God," before continuing. Why? After listening to the Scriptures for six hours and discerning the living voice of God in what they heard, the people were able to perceive the greatness of God, along with his holy, merciful, gracious, and loving character.

This rhema teaching allowed them to witness God's treatment of Israel over time. They heard how he delivered them through great acts of power; how he guarded them and protected them, and continuously forgave them for their rebellion and sin. They realized that in his mercy, he had extended a law that revealed his character and that made a way for them to live in closeness to him.

After all that revelation, they could no longer just call him "God"; in their elevated perspective, he had become the "Great God!" So they blessed the Great God in unity; hence, "Amen, Amen," as they all captured the same revelation and bowed before him. And even after six hours of standing and listening to the Book of the Law read, they moved into sincere worship!

Today, many sectors of Christianity have lost sight of God's heart and essence. While quite familiar with the rituals of worship, we have lost focus on the deity we are offering our worship to. We lost our sense of awe for God and have taken him for granted; in many instances our worship has deteriorated into an empty custom.

Hence, the importance of arriving at the Water Gate - God's glory, character, and might are illuminated to us through Scripture, and we realize his greatness and it overshadows our humanity. At that moment, we share the perspective of David when he wrote in

Psalm 8:4, "What is man that you are mindful of him, and the son of man that you visit him?" (NKJV)

Our elevated perspective of him causes us to fall face down to the ground in humility, love, awe, and reverence as we recognize how twisted our perspective of him has been; and how little we deserve to be favored by such an amazing God. In elevation, we recognize the sacrifice God made in order to even permit us into his presence and allow us to render our sacrifices of praise.

The Water Gate Revealed in the New Testament

With all that we've learned from Nehemiah 8 regarding true spiritual elevation, let's turn our attention to the New Testament. Here we will notice similar outcomes the disciples experienced when Christ sent them to higher ground and experienced spiritual elevation

Take a look at this familiar Scripture:

> *Then they returned to Jerusalem from the mountain called the Mount of Olives (which is near Jerusalem, a Sabbath day's journey away). When they had entered Jerusalem, they went to the <u>upstairs room</u> where they were staying. Peter and John, James, and Andrew, Philip and Thomas, Bartholomew and Matthew, James son of Alphaeus and Simon the Zealot, and Judas son of James were there. All these continued together in prayer with one mind, together with the women, along with Mary the mother of Jesus, and his brothers. (Acts 1:12-14)*

The disciples, after receiving Christ's instructions and witnessing him ascend to the Father (Acts 1:1-11), went back to Jerusalem and returned to their former lodgings.

After that, the disciples no longer debated over the identity of Christ. They chose, instead, to focus on the marvels they had witnessed; Christ's directives and his intended purposes also took precedence. As a result, they found themselves ready for spiritual elevation. And just as one would have to climb up the stairs of the ascending wall in Jerusalem to get to the Water Gate, the disciple's room required them to walk upstairs in order to get there; we all know that particular room as "The Upper Room". That elevated room would also become their "Water Gate".

While they tarried and waited as they had been instructed, they stayed constant in prayer and in *one accord*!

> *And when the day of Pentecost was fully come, they were all with one accord in one place.*

(Acts 2:1 KJV)

Here we see unity, one of the characteristics we read about at the Water Gate, taking place at an elevated location.

On the Day of Pentecost, Christ kept his promise to send the Holy Spirit. The Spirit descended on the Holy Day of Pentecost on those gathered in the Upper Room, indwelling and empowering them to be effective witnesses for him. Many of those present in Jerusalem came from other countries. To their astonishment, after the Holy Spirit fell on the disciples, these people heard the latter declaring the wonders of God in their own particular languages.

The people felt astonishment because they recognized the disciples were Galileans who didn't speak the foreign languages spoken by those present who were visiting from other countries. Some, however, mocked them and accused them of being drunk, but observe Peter's response to this accusation in Acts 2:14-35 (AKJ):

> *But Peter standing up with the eleven, lifted up his voice, and said to them, You men of Judaea, and all you that dwell at Jerusalem, be this known to you, and listen to my words: For these are not drunken, as you suppose, seeing it is but the third hour of the day. But this is that which was spoken by*

the prophet Joel; And it shall come to pass in the last days, says God, I will pour out of my Spirit upon all flesh: and your sons and your daughters will prophesy, and your young men will see visions, and your old men will dream dreams. And on my servants and on my handmaidens I will pour out in those days of my Spirit; and they will prophesy. And I will show wonders in heaven above, and signs in the earth beneath; blood, and fire, and vapor of smoke: The sun will be turned into darkness, and the moon into blood, before the great and notable day of the Lord come: And it will come to pass, that whosoever will call on the name of the Lord, will be saved. You men of Israel, hear these words; Jesus of Nazareth, a man approved of God among you by miracles and wonders and signs, which God did by him in the midst of you, as you yourselves also know: Him being delivered by the determinate counsel and foreknowledge of God, you have taken and by wicked hands have crucified and slain: Whom God has raised up, having loosed the pains of death: because it was not possible that he should be held of it. For David speaks concerning him, I foresaw the Lord always before my face. For he is on my right hand, that I should not be moved: Therefore did my heart rejoice, and my tongue was glad; moreover also my flesh will rest in hope: Because you will not leave my soul in hell, neither will you suffer your Holy One to see corruption. You have made known to me the ways of life; you will make me full of joy with your countenance. Men and brothers, let me freely speak to you of the patriarch David, that he is both dead and buried, and his sepulcher is with us to this day. Therefore being a prophet, and knowing that God had sworn with an oath to him, that of the fruit of his loins, according to the flesh, he would raise up Christ to sit his throne; He seeing this before spoke of the resurrection of Christ, that his soul was not left in hell, neither his flesh did see corruption. This Jesus has God raised up, whereof we all are witnesses. Therefore being by the right hand of God exalted, and having received of the Father the promise of the Holy Ghost, he has shed forth this, which you now see and hear. For David is not ascended into the heavens: but he said himself, The LORD said to my Lord, Sit you on my right hand, until I make your foes your footstool.

How remarkable! This same Peter who cowardly denied any relationship with Jesus after his arrest, now possessed the courage to openly preach his Savior before the multitudes! Emboldened by the Holy Spirit to stand before the assembly, Peter began his discourse by saying, "Hearken to my words."

Guess what word in the Greek language actually means "words" in this passage? *Rhema*! Peter actually said "Listen to my *rhema* – the living voice of God in what I'm about to say." And what did he do next? He began giving the proper meaning to prophecies from the prophet Joel and King David so that the people present could understand the divine moment they were living in and experiencing – the time for Reconciliation with God!

But who instructed Peter on the exact meaning of those prophetic Scriptures found in the Torah? The Holy Spirit did, of course, as all of the disciples arrived at their personal "Water Gate"—the gate of elevation!

If you recall, John 7:37-39 states:

> *In the last day, that great day of the feast, Jesus stood and cried, saying, if any man thirst, let him come unto me, and drink. He that believeth on me, as the Scripture hath said, out of his belly shall flow rivers of living water. (But this spake he of the Spirit, which they that believe on him should receive: for the Holy Ghost was not yet given; because that Jesus was not yet glorified). (KJV)*

Christ likened the Holy Spirit to water. The moment finally came when Christ poured out that water he promised once he was glorified! They were experiencing the revelation of the Water Gate which began at the elevated place of the Upper Room! Once that

Water from heaven, the Holy Spirit, was poured out on them, He empowered them with the essential characteristics, attributes, and abilities to make reconciliation between God and man conducive and possible. The Holy Spirit enabled them to understand and explain the true meaning of the Scripture. This *rhema* produced faith in the hearts of the people, and many repented and turned back to the living God. And so that you can see that even at the time of Nehemiah spiritual elevation had everything to do with preparing a people for reconciliation, notice what the people did the day after their experience in Nehemiah 8 that we discussed earlier:

> *On the second day of the month the family leaders met with Ezra the scribe, together with all the people, the priests, and the Levites, to consider the words of the law. They discovered written in the law that the Lord had commanded through Moses that the Israelites should live in temporary shelters during the festival of the seventh month, and that they should make a proclamation and disseminate this message in all their cities and in Jerusalem: "Go to the hill country and bring back olive branches and branches of wild olive trees, myrtle trees, date palms, and other leafy trees to construct temporary shelters, as it is written."... So all the assembly which had returned from the exile constructed temporary shelters and lived in them. The Israelites had not done so from the days of Joshua son of Nun until that day. Everyone experienced very great joy. Ezra read in the book of the law of God day by day, form the first day to the last. They observed the festival for seven days, and on the eighth day they held an assembly as was required. (Nehemiah 8:13-15; 17-18)*

Amazing! The day after this great experience at the Water Gate, the family leaders met with Ezra, priests, and Levites. Together, they discovered that God had commanded a feast called the Feast of Tabernacles. God instructed his people to hold the feast for a seven day period; during that time the people lived in temporal shelters they constructed to symbolize God and his people dwelling together! The gate of Spiritual Elevation will always result in people being reconciled to God, and his church preparing to dwell with him for eternity!

Often times, people interpret the ultimate purpose of elevation to be an increase in miracles, signs, and wonders. I want to encourage Christians to not become distracted with the different signs and wonders the disciples experienced on the day of Pentecost. God used these tools to effectively communicate the things most important to him: the gospel, and the accurate interpretation and presentation of the Word of God that validates it. This resulted in faith, repentance, and reconciliation with God among the people.

At this point in our journey, we live in divine unity with our brothers and sisters in Christ; have obtained a proper perspective of the Word of God; understand that the whole of it has to do with reconciliation and restoration to God; the Word has become the supreme authority of our lives; and our perception, perspective, and worship of God is elevated. We can now proceed to journey onward to the Horse Gate - the gate of spiritual warfare.

THE HORSE GATE (PART 1)

When we read about horses in Bible stories, they almost exclusively relate or refer to war or armies. Among other factors, this information proves useful in determining that spiritual warfare represents the essential meaning of the Horse Gate. This chapter purposes to convey the Biblical perspective of spiritual warfare so that we can engage in it as God intends and experience a victorious outcome.

The Reason for Warfare

War can be described as an armed and open, hostile conflict between nations. In Christianity, the kingdom of Satan continually exists in a declared, antagonistic battle with the kingdom of God. In order to perceive spiritual warfare from God's point of view, we have to understand the precise purpose for the warfare and the parties involved. The Bible states that Satan, God's archenemy, prowls around like a lion, not only seeking someone to devour, but also to destroy the advancement of God's empire. That explains why the gate of warfare immediately follows the Water Gate, the gate of elevation. Here our understanding of God's Word took on a new dimension, and we became very skilled at communicating the Gospel. Only this message effectively advances the kingdom of God which makes reconciliation with him possible. The Gospel supplies the only means by which God's kingdom and influence grow and weakens Satan's control and power.

The Word of Truth: Satan's Greatest Threat

Nothing can more greatly impact Satan's kingdom than the accurate and rightly-divided Word of truth and the message of the gospel. In response, the adversary turns up the heat on those preaching the message, in a desperate attempt to silence this report.

Look at the disciples. When they arrived at their spiritual Water Gate on the Day of Pentecost, they were filled with the water from heaven, the Holy Spirit. This enabled them to give the accurate meaning to the Old Testament Scriptures and caused their listeners to see Christ as Messiah; to understand that his work on the cross was for mankind's reconciliation with God and would lead many to repentance. This brought about a huge backlash of persecution and death from the enemy.

Previously, Satan simply tempted them, but at the first sight of effective kingdom advancement, he began to attack the Christians more aggressively. Revelation 6:9 further proves this point and provides insight for why Christians may suffer persecution:

> *Now when the Lamb opened the fifth seal, I saw under the altar the souls of those who had been violently killed because of the word of God and because of the testimony they had given.*

This verse reveals the reason many will be martyred in end-times— they will be put to death because of the Word of God they preach and their testimony, meaning the uncompromising life of holiness they live.

While Satan has frequently employed the use of martyrdom and torture in his effort to halt the forward movement of God's domain, he has also used other methods to impede God from gaining followers through the message of truth. In the Parable of the Sower in Matthew 13, Mark 4, and Luke 8, we learn that when faced with God's true word, Satan desperately attempts to snatch or choke it out of the lives of individuals who hear it – again, the attack is in response the true Word of God.

Although martyrdom and torture are certainly options Satan employs as much as possible, his more common method at attempting to hinder the advancement of God's kingdom is deception. We first see an example of this in the Garden of Eden. God commanded Adam not to eat from the Tree of the Knowledge of Good and Evil or he would die; Satan, embodied in a serpent, caused Eve to question and doubt the word God spoke to them.

Satan succeeded in creating enough doubt and lured Eve into sin. Subsequently, Adam followed suit.

Satan is committed to distort our perspective of the Word of God so that we misapply it, create false rumors, or teachings, of it, and twist it in order to make it ineffective in our lives and the lives of those we preach it to. Remember, a Scripture misinterpreted and misapplied is powerless and ineffective.

In like manner, when Christ was baptized, the Father testified of his pleasure with Jesus, his son. Immediately after, the Spirit led Christ into the wilderness where Satan tempted him for forty days. He unsuccessfully tried to duplicate the same doubt about God's Word in Christ that he had sowed into Adam and Eve in the Garden. They succumbed to sin but Jesus did not. He recognized the devil's attempts to distort Scripture, presenting it out of context and devoid of God's intended purpose. Christ understood that Satan only wanted to invalidate his authority to create a way of salvation for fallen humanity (Matthew 4:1-11).

The State of the Church in End-Time Warfare

As we move forward, you must keep in mind that the sole purpose behind Satan's vicious attacks against the body of Christ lies in his desire to sabotage and prevent the growth of God's kingdom through reconciliation; and to cause those already a part of it to renounce Christ, or apostatize, and turn away. Therefore, we must remain aware of the proven tactics mentioned above that Satan has consistently used to try and accomplish his goal.

Aware now of Satan's motives and tactics, we will advance through the gate of spiritual warfare and approach it from two fronts. First, we will provide an overview of the horses found in Revelation chapter 6, as they will help us understand the state of the different sectors of the Church in end-time warfare; and then, we will study closely many of the Scriptures often used and misinterpreted when discussing spiritual warfare. We will unpack those Scriptures with the hope of making us more effective in our approach in this important aspect of our Christian walk.

The White Horse

It is important to note that in prophecy horses signify groups of people. Revelation chapter 6 makes the reader aware of four prominent groups that will be present in end-times near the Second Coming of our Lord. In this chapter, the groups of people are symbolized by the horses.

> *I looked on when the Lamb opened one of the seven seals, and I heard one of the four living creatures saying with a thunderous voice, "Come!" So I looked, and here came a white horse! The one who rode it had a bow, and he was given a crown, and as a conqueror he rode out to conquer. (Verses 1, 2)*

The white horse in verse one symbolizes the company of people who have taken on the character of Jesus Christ in end-times. These individuals have washed their robes in the blood of the lamb and have put on the robe of righteousness (Revelation 7:14) – those whose characters have been transformed into righteous ones by accepting the work of Jesus on the cross. Although some outlooks believe this person riding the white horse to be the antichrist, an in-depth study of the Scriptures will reveal that it is actually Christ himself. Those in this group will be ridden, or utilized, by Christ in the last days; conquering the kingdom of darkness with the Word of Truth, a sword that symbolizes the Word of God (Ephesians 6:17).

Then when the Lamb opened the second seal, I heard the second living creature saying, "Come!" And another horse, fiery red, came out, and the one who rode it was granted permission to take peace from the earth, so that people would butcher one another, and he was given a huge sword. (Verses 3, 4)

This fiery red horse denotes the apostate church at the end of time. This sector of the church turns away from the truth and follows false doctrine or false teaching.

But how would an apostate church take peace from the earth through false teaching? To understand this, we must be clear on what kind of peace the above verse refers to. Could it be the absence of stress and worry? Perhaps, the absence of trouble and warfare? No. When God speaks of peace, he often refers to one particular kind of peace; the peace between God and man – this is the peace that the gospel promotes. The prophetic Scriptures of Isaiah 53:5 referred to this peace when speaking of Christ: "…the punishment that brought us peace was on him…" (NIV).

The book of Romans makes clear the enmity prevailing between fallen humanity and our Creator. No longer enemies of God because of our sin, we become the righteousness of God thanks to Christ, who through His death made a way for God to make peace with man. That is why the prophet Isaiah refers to him as the Prince of Peace (Isaiah 9:6).

Furthermore, at the birth of Christ an angel appeared to nearby shepherds, proclaiming the good news of the Messiah's birth. Then, "suddenly there was with the angel a multitude of the heavenly host praising God, and saying, 'Glory to God in the highest, and on earth peace, good will toward men'" (Luke 2:13-14). The heavenly host loudly declared that the Savior, the Prince of Peace, had arrived on earth to make a way for God and man to be reconciled. This meant an end to the hostility between God and man because Christ not only paid the penalty of sin, but also made the forgiveness of sin possible. As a result, the message of Christ's death, burial, and resurrection, which made forgiveness of sin possible, is the Gospel, or good news; or as Ephesians 6:15 calls it, the *"gospel of peace"*, the catalyst to bring peace on earth between humanity and God.

Satan intends to prevent this gospel of peace from going forth by relying heavily on his most used method - deceiving the church into preaching a different message. Since the Church operates as God's vehicle to deliver the message of peace to the world, getting the Church to replace the gospel with something else would accomplish Satan's goal of preventing peace between God and man.

Satan understands that in order to compel the Church to preach a message other than the true gospel, the new message would have to be engaging, compelling, and attractive. So far, Satan has been able to accomplish this in various circles of Christianity, pushing excessive humanistic messages focused on finding happiness on earth by achieving personal goals and dreams; sermons that encourage making peace with oneself, becoming emotionally healthy and financially prosperous. What's not to like? On the surface, they seem to be things that the church should address. On the flip side, Satan can accomplish the same with legalistic teachings or messages that deal heavily with signs, wonders, and the supernatural. Something is drastically wrong when the message of redemption and reconciliation are replaced with constant sermons of prosperity, self-help, and miracles, signs, and wonders. Peace cannot exist outside of anything other than the atoning work of Christ and sanctification.

How False Teaching Thrives in the Church

When we read Revelation chapters two and three, we find that Christ had a message for seven churches located in Asia.

Those churches represent the seven different sectors of the body of Christ that will be present in end-times. To the church in Pergamum and Thyatira, Christ first addressed what pleased him about them. In his address to Pergamum, Christ recognized their commitment to cling to his name and not deny their faith; when addressing Thyatira, he acknowledged their love, faith, service, and steadfast endurance.

However, despite having such great qualities, they both shared a similar attribute that greatly displeased him: both churches allowed false teachers to spread false doctrines in their congregations which caused people to stumble and fall away. Christ called those false doctrines the teachings of Balaam, the Nicolaitans, and Jezebel. Many components, similar in substance, could be found in all three teachings. They condoned sexual immorality and food that had been sacrificed to idols. Christ strongly warned against such doctrines, giving them a <u>short</u> time to repent or he would bring judgment against those that followed such teachers and teachings.

Let's stop for a moment and ask, "How could churches that demonstrated such great characteristics, qualities, and commitment allow these false teachers into their church, much less exposing their people to such immoral and unethical teachings? As readers, we may even stop to think, "Obviously God speaks out against immorality, so how could such deplorable doctrines be tolerated and followed?" To better understand how false doctrine can thrive among believers, we have to look at Jezebel.

This Jezebel, married to Israel's King Ahab, led the Israelites into idol worship on a massive scale; Christ condemned the false teachers in the church of Thyatira for polluting his Gospel with her demonic propaganda. (You can further study more about Jezebel in the story found in 1 Kings).

Her position gave her power and influence which she leveraged to persuade the King to worship her pagan gods and to promote such worship among the worshippers of Yahweh, the living God.

Jezebel further used her status and influence to order the killings of many true prophets of God because she wanted to shut the voices of truth. Sadly, without the voices of truth, the people followed Ahab into idolatry.

In Revelation 2:13, Christ calls Pergamum the throne or seat of Satan because of his strong influence there. The impact of his sway in this city, resulted in the death of Antipas, whom Christ considered to be a faithful witness; he not only spoke the truth of God's Word, he also lived it. Notice what came after Antipas' death according to Christ's letter to the church: false teaching.

The death of Antipas enabled Satan to influence the teachers of that church who came after him. Those teachers entertained false doctrine, until finally, they were indoctrinating the church with Balaam's reprehensible, sacrilegious message.

Balaam was a prophet who prophesied the Oracles of God in the Old Testament. The king of Moab, the enemy of Israel, paid Balaam a lucrative amount of money to get him to curse the people of God in order to defeat them. Although Balaam, in "obedience" to God, would not curse Israel, he sorely desired to because he coveted the money and riches the king of Moab provided him (2 Peter 2:15). Balaam soon recognized the need to change his strategy in order to keep the finances coming. He decided to tell the enemy how to get the people to curse themselves. Balaam advised the king to send the Moabite women near the men of Israel, and sooner or later, the women would be successful in enticing the men to sleep with them (Numbers 31:8-18). It worked and, soon after, the men of Israel committed sexual immorality with the Moabite women; they also began to worship their false gods (Numbers 25).

God had already made it very clear to the Israelites that he detested idol worship; he found it abominable and warned that those practicing it would face his judgment and wrath; the Israelites ended up cursing themselves through sin, as it caused God's favor to be taken from them.

This perfectly demonstrates how Satan, like a roaring lion, seeks to devour the church, by eliminating the voices of truth. Sometimes, in his craftiness, Satan may open the door for influential church leaders to connect and work with people in the secular world. The devil hopes to use this "promising" union to strip church leaders of their spiritual vision. If Satan can accomplish stealing the church leader's vision, that leader will deviate from the message of truth and lead his church astray. This parallels Ahab's experience with Jezebel after he married her and made her queen of Israel. She used her hold on the king in order to seduce him into her sinful practices.

As he did with Balaam, Satan continues to use riches to draw influential church leaders into false teachings. Many preachers of the gospel come from humble beginnings and limited recourses; this makes it easy for Satan to persuade them to exchange truth and godliness for financial gain. Their messages are compelling, and even, appear to be backed by Scripture. Possibly these men of God may have even fooled themselves into believing their teachings hold up to biblical standards but a close investigation soon negates the probability of that premise. A more thorough investigation will demonstrate the fallacy of such teachings, erroneous messages lacking the breath of God that lead God's people into apostasy. Peter warns us to beware of this in his epistle, urging us to be sober-minded and alert (1 Peter 5:8).

When his disciples asked him to give them a sign of the endtimes, Christ responded with, "Watch out that no one misleads, or deceives, you," (Matthew 24:4). Why? Christ knew that Satan would raise up great speakers with a rhetoric powerful enough to manipulate Scripture and lead people astray with false teachings. But what further enhances the power of deception is what Paul refers to as people with "itching ears" – or wanting to hear what is pleasing to their flesh (2 Timothy 4:3). Notice what the full verse says:

For the time will come when people will not put up with sound doctrine. Instead, to suit their own desires, they will gather around them a great number of teachers to say what their itching ears want to hear. (NIV)

Thankfully, Christ gave us an example in resisting such temptation, and the apostle Peter, who reminded us to be sober and alert, was a firsthand witness. When Peter was used by Satan to try and dissuade Christ from going to the Cross, it sounded good and even resonated with Christ's desire not to go. However, Christ refused, being sober, alert, and willing to obey his Father in all things. He looked at Peter and said, "Get behind me, Satan! You are a stumbling block to me because you are not setting your mind on God's interests, but on man's," (Matthew 16:21-23).

Peter learned that Satan had a crafty way of presenting carnal and humanistic messages that gratify the flesh, as truth. As mentioned in previous chapters, if Satan can accomplish getting people to follow false teachings, he knows it will ultimately lead to their destruction, and having itching ears makes a person more susceptible to falsehood.

The Black Horse: The Group that Repents

As mentioned before, Christ's message to the two churches in Revelation, demonstrated that possessing godly qualities cannot negate the ultimate judgment from God for those who continue in falsehood. The good news remains that those proclaiming the pure and true message of the White Horse in Revelation 6, greatly influence many followers of the Red Horse; they persuade those represented by the latter horse to repent; the Black Horse symbolizes the people who repented.

Notice what the Scriptures say about the Black Horse:

Then when the Lamb opened the third seal I heard the third living creature saying, "Come!" So I looked, and here came a black horse! The one who rode it had a balance scale in his hand. Then I heard something like a voice from among the four living creatures saying, "A quart of wheat will cost a day's pay and three quarts of barley will cost a day's pay. But do not damage the olive oil and the wine!"(Verses 5, 6)

Who would be willing to work a full day just to earn enough to buy a small quart of wheat or three quarts of barley? Certainly no one making a decent living with a full stomach and a roof over their head would work for that type of wage. However, what if we asked someone living in a land of famine and starving to death if they would work an entire day in exchange for a quart of wheat or three quarts of barley to make bread? Would they be willing to put in a full day's work for so little in return? Of course they would! Their only question would be, "What work must I do?"

In the same manner, at the end of the age, many will fall prey to erroneous and false teachings. A steady diet of this will result in a famine of the true Word of God. Those hungry enough for the truth will be willing to forsake these false teachings and do whatever it takes to get their hands on this bread from heaven.

The Spirit of God, represented by the oil and the wine, will continue his work of sanctification in the lives of those who repent and reconnect with the true Word of God.

The Pale Horse of Martyrdom

Upon the "re-gathering" work of the white horse of the many Christians from apostasy, we see the Pale Horse of persecution and martyrdom present itself.

Then when the Lamb opened the fourth seal I heard the voice of the fourth living creature saying, "Come!" So I looked and here came a pale green horse! The name of the one who rode it was Death, and Hades followed right behind. They were given authority over a fourth of the earth, to kill its population with the sword, famine, and disease, and by the wild animals of the earth. (Verses 7, 8)

As noted above, the group symbolized by the pale horse will seek to kill the saints who maintain the truth of the Word of God and their witness through a holy lifestyle.

As in the case of Antipas and the disciples after Pentecost, this group will seek out and pursue the effective saints who are effectively spreading the Word of Truth, in order to shut their message.

Again, I want to highlight that in the history of the Bible, the prophets of God and Christians who faced persecution did so for two reasons: the Word of Truth they spoke and their refusal to compromise their holy lifestyle. So when learning and teaching about warfare, this fact must be kept foremost in order to properly understand the subject and not be distracted by strange ideas that we will investigate in the next chapter, The Horse Gate Part 2.

THE HORSE GATE (PART 2)

Today it is easy to find people who say God has revealed great mysteries to them about the spiritual world through visions, dreams, and prophecies. How do we separate fact from fiction with so many people making so many bold assertions? What method do we use to sift through the many voices and determine which is in accordance with God? Well, let's search the Scriptures to see what they teach us.

Let's begin by first determining what sort of people God chooses to impart these deeper understandings of spiritual matters to, as they relate to true warfare.

Daniel 9:20-23(AJV) helps highlight the precedent God set in order for him to give someone the privilege of understanding such mysteries – they would have to be greatly beloved, or as another version of the Bible puts it, highly-esteemed.

> *And whiles I was speaking, and praying, and confessing my sin and the sin of my people Israel, and presenting my supplication before the LORD my God for the holy mountain of my God; Yes, whiles I was speaking in prayer, even the man Gabriel, whom I had seen in the vision at the beginning, being caused to fly swiftly, touched me about the time of the evening oblation.*
>
> *And he informed me, and talked with me, and said, O Daniel, I am now come forth to give you skill and understanding. At the beginning of thy supplications the commandment came forth, and I am come to show you; for you are greatly beloved: therefore understand the matter, and consider the vision.*

To be greatly beloved does not mean that He loves certain Chris-

tians more than others. One way to look at it, to better understand, is from a parent's perspective.

For the most part, we, as parents, love all of our children with an
immeasurable love; however, we may have a closer relationship
with one child over the others because they interact with us more
often. They frequently call us, express affection for us and concern themselves with our needs and wants. Simply put, they more
regularly demonstrate their love for us compared to the others so
we would probably seek them out first when something important
should arise because of the closeness of our relationship. This same
principle made Daniel highly-esteemed in the eyes of God.

The prophet Daniel was a man taken captive into Babylonian exile
during Babylon's first wave of attack against Judah in 605 B.C. While
in captivity, Daniel, who had lived a life of devotion in Judah, continued to dedicate himself to God in Babylon, and even when faced
with death, Daniel chose to die rather than sin against God through
compromise. Daniel's obedience and commitment to God landed
him in a den of lions as a death sentence, and yet, he did not waiver.

Because Daniel set his love and devotion on the Most High, God
looked upon him with favor, affectionately addressing him as his
greatly beloved. For this particular reason, God elected to reveal
these end-time mysteries to his greatly beloved servant, Daniel.

Similarly, the disciple John, also spoke of himself as the one whom
Jesus loved, while writing his Gospel. In his book, John points
to specific moments and occasions that offer us a glimpse of the
bond he shared with Christ. The longest living disciple, he suffered enormous persecution for the sake of the Lord. The early
Christian theologian and author, Tertullian, described how, on
one occasion, the Roman soldiers plunged John into boiling oil.
According to the author, John did not die, so the Emperor Domi-
tian banished him to the island of Patmos. His close commitment
to Christ produced a long life full of obedience and faithfulness,
even at the cost of his own. It also gave God a vessel that he could

reveal and entrust with great end-time visions and prophecies as well.

While we may all desire to be so highly thought of, only those with an uncompromising commitment to God and his Word, will ever achieve such status. Once a person is greatly beloved by God, it makes them a part of the group who God can disclose his divine mysteries to as they pertain to spiritual matters occurring in the heavenly realms and on earth. Coupled with that, God wants us to rest assured that whatever he reveals to us, he also wants us to understand. Some hold to the notion that God gives prophetic words, dreams, or visions deliberately shrouded in mystery, the meaning of them to remain obscure or vague. They don't realize that, God wants to ensure that we have the understanding of their meaning. Look at the following passage which reinforces this fact:

> And, behold, a hand touched me, which set me on my knees and upon the palms of my hands. And he said to me, O Daniel, a man greatly beloved, understand the words that I speak to you, and stand upright: for to you am I now sent. And when he had spoken this word to me, I stood trembling. Then he said to me, Fear not, Daniel: for from the first day that you set your heart to understand, and to chasten yourself before your God, your words were heard, and I am come for your words. But the prince of the kingdom of Persia withstood me one and twenty days: but, lo, Michael, one of the chief princes, came to help me; and I remained there with the kings of Persia. Now I am come to make you understand what will befall your people in the latter days: for yet the vision is for many days. (Daniel 10:10-14, AKJ)

Simply put, God wants his people to know him! In fact, he wants us to understand the meaning of what he shows us more than we want it. In the above passage, we read that the angel had been sent to Daniel, specifically, to give him understanding of the vision; and this is not the only time we see this occur with Daniel. You see, it does not please God to show us a vision or a dream, or give us a prophetic word and not give us the understand of it. Especially for those who arrive to the Horse Gate since, spiritually, such person has been to the Water Gate and received a God-given passion to understand the truth of his Word. At this point in the journey, a person will not be satisfied simply with hearing a prophetic word or seeing a vision or dream, but they also want to understand the meaning – and God wants to reveal it.

So beware of those unable to ever interpret or provide the actual meaning of the dreams and visions allegedly given to them by God. Kindly ask them to not share it until God provides the understanding.

Also, remember this important point: in a true revelation from heaven, the meaning will always align, and must always align, with the Word of God—the Scriptures. While this sounds like common knowledge, the truth is, there is so much that has been allowed to be said to the body of Christ by many who profess to have a word from God, but don't. Often, their erroneous and deceptive messages and "private interpretations" are embraced by people with itching ears who disregard weighing whether their words are true, according to the Word of God. To avoid this pitfall, Christians must have a thorough understanding of Scripture – and that is each Christian's personal responsibility (2 Timothy 2:15).

Characteristics of a Person who has seen the Glorified Christ

Popularity plays a huge role in leading so many astray. Many regard those delivering erroneous and false messages as "highly anointed" – sometimes because the person may be a renowned figure – and absolve the person from any responsibility and accountability to the truth of the Scriptures. After the following passage, I want to share an example of a testimony given by a well-renowned preacher who said he was taken up to heaven and met with Jesus.

In the third year of King Cyrus of Persia a message was re-

vealed to Daniel (who was also called Belteshazzar). This message was true and concerned a great war. He understood the message and gained insight by the vision. In those days I, Daniel, was mourning for three whole weeks. I ate no choice food; no meat or wine came to my lips, nor did I anoint myself with oil until the end of those three weeks. On the twenty-fourth day of the first month I was beside the great river, the Tigris. I looked up and saw a man clothed in linen; around his waist was a belt made of gold from Upaz. His body resembled yellow jasper, and his face had an appearance like lightning. His eyes were like blazing torches; his arms and feet had the gleam of polished bronze. His voice thundered forth like the sound of a large crowd. Only I, Daniel, saw the vision; the men who were with me did not see it. On the contrary, they were overcome with fright and ran away to hide. I alone was left to see this great vision. My strength drained from me, and my vigor disappeared; I was without energy. I listened to his voice, and as I did so I fell into a trance-like sleep with my face to the ground. Then a hand touched me and set me on my hands and knees. He said to me, "Daniel, you are of great value. Understand the words that I am about to speak to you. So stand up, for I have now been sent to you." When he said this to me, I stood up shaking. (Daniel 10:1-11, KJV)

Here's the example I'd like to share. One day I listened to a well-renowned preacher, who I admired and whose teachings I enjoyed. He gave a testimony about how God took them up to heaven. According to the preacher's testimony, Christ gave them a tour of heaven. The preacher was even shown a "warehouse," or room, that stored a great number of gifts that had not been claimed by Christians on earth because of their lack of belief to receive them. When the preacher came back to himself on earth, he had been burdened with the task of admonishing the body of Christ to claim every blessing God had in store for them, and in the context of what he was saying, it was mainly material "blessings."

Excited by the message, I completely believed what he said; after all, lots of Christians bragged about his "powerful anointing" so he could certainly be trusted, right? Like that preacher, many people boldly declare that they have met with Jesus and that he has personally given them a message. While I will never limit God, I do want to address a couple of things: first, what does Scripture tell us about the person making these declarations? What spiritual characteristics should we look for in such a person? Secondly, what would be the message of someone who really encountered the glorified Son.

Daniel, the beloved prophet, actually had a vision of Jesus Christ, the glorified Son of God, dressed in white linen. How do we know? We know because Daniel's vision of the divine person he saw closely parallels the same description of Christ given by John in the book of Revelation.

Only Daniel saw this vision in the above verse, because he was the one who was greatly beloved, or highly-esteemed; the men with him did not see it.

The moment Daniel saw Christ, he *lost his strength* and *felt helpless* – not hopeful, but helpless. The vision of the glorified savior caused him to *turn deathly pale* and *lose consciousness*. Even after being helped up, Daniel *trembled* and *was afraid*. That was the reaction of a man who had lived upright and pleasing to God and was regarded as greatly beloved!

Likewise, John the Revelator, after seeing the glorified Christ, wrote in Revelation 1:17:

> *When I saw him I fell down at his feet as though I were dead, but he placed his right hand on me and said: "Do not be afraid! I am the first and the last."*

This same John, a disciple of Christ, walked and interacted with him daily. Once glorified, even John, despite the relationship he had with him on earth, could not casually look at Him, but instead, felt *overwhelmed* and *afraid* in his presence.

We need to consider these details since we repeatedly hear testimonies from people discussing their encounters and conversations with Christ. Those who casually or even boastfully speak of these "appointments" should not be taken seriously no matter how mystical it may sound or how peppered with supernatural language it may be.

No one, irrespective of their fame or anointing, can ever walk away from an encounter with Christ without reacting in much the same way that such proven men, like Daniel or John, did in similar circumstances.

Even Paul, formerly known as Saul, fell off his mount and lost his sight after crossing paths with Christ. This encounter humbled and changed him from Saul, the persecutor of Christians, into someone greatly beloved by God.

Now, I am not referring to the leading of the Spirit; I'm talking about encountering the manifested, ascended Savior. No flesh can stand before him, no matter how anointed or renowned the person. In fact, Scripture tells us that those who experience such encounters become so overwhelmed that they fall to their knees. So when men or women speak so nonchalantly of these divine instances, rest assured they have not met with Christ or received any genuine revelation.

Our experience at the Water Gate teaches us to put more weight on the Scriptures, rather than, biblically unfounded, emotionally driven testimonies and teachings of preachers, whether famous or not. Once I began establishing my beliefs based solely on Scripture, I realized that no one could be transported to heaven, returned to earth, and just casually talk about it. Furthermore, the message certainly would contain no mention of unimportant temporal blessings, but would sound more like, "I saw the glorified

King! Oh my God, I saw the glorified King and I almost died but he strengthened me." Such an experience would explode with a message of eternal value that relates to the message God has been conveying for millennia; the reconciliation of man through Christ and an urgency to spread the message and prepare for Christ's Second Coming.

Where in Scripture, can we locate any verses that support the preacher's vision concerning the unclaimed gifts? Nowhere did John even remotely touch upon these things in the Book of Revelation. Christ's messages to the end-time churches make no mention of people not receiving their blessings before leaving earth. And most certainly, there are no mentions of rooms with unclaimed blessings in heaven. Therefore, when weighing such testimony against the Word of God, it cannot be accepted as truth. Therefore, plainly speaking, no one living in this earthly body can stand before the physical manifestation of Christ and not be significantly affected by it. Again, testimonies like these cannot be accepted as truth if they do not align with the Word of Truth.

The Christian's Approach to Satan in Warfare

As we move further in this lesson, I want to stress that any passage of Scripture we study moving forward will be addressed as it relates to Satan, the archenemy of our faith. I will not discuss evil spirits in this chapter. Evil spirits have their place in warfare and I look forward to discussing them in a separate publication. I find their role and characteristics important to study, as many have often diagnosed the works of the flesh as evil spirits. Unless we can properly distinguish between evil spirits and the works of the flesh, we will likely be ineffective in our ministry in this aspect of warfare as we will often confuse the two and apply the wrong remedy to the wrong problem. The separate publication will help identify the differences. Once we can identify, for certain, an evil spirit, the Bible offers clear instructions what to do.

As for Satan, our nemesis, many Christians fail to understand the methods in which the Bible instructs us to properly and effectively engage him in spiritual warfare. Many have rebuked Satan, bound him and commanded him to go back to the pit of hell. Others have pleaded or applied the blood of Jesus, symbolically, around their homes and churches to prevent him from entering in. And still, others have anointed their homes and the apparel of their loved ones with oil in order to keep him away from them. But does Scripture actually endorse these tactics as adequate strategies for engaging in spiritual conflict? By the time we reach the close of this chapter, I feel confident that you will certainly comprehend Yahweh's established methods for Christian warfare, specifically, against Satan.

In many circles of Christianity, strong belief systems based on emotionalism and mysticism have been established as modes for dealing with Satan. Many of those practices conflict with Scripture so the Bible does not support them. One example involves the approach of binding Satan and casting him back "to the pit of hell where he came from."

While this approach may sound biblical and like a classic "What Would Jesus Do" type of situation, we need to take a better look at the validity of this formula. I used to live by this method for many years since it made so much sense to me. It wasn't until I reached the Water Gate in my journey and investigated the Scriptures thoroughly, that I realized the holes in the second part of that approach. I came to understand that by simply putting together a few verses, the idea of casting Satan back into the pit of hell "from whence he came," could easily be debunked; and I will show you how, momentarily.

Let me provide some background on Satan to establish some vital context. Originally, Satan held the position of the highest-ranking angel in heaven, known as Lucifer, meaning, *morning star* (Isaiah 14:12-14). The Bible says that he practically epitomized the seal of perfection, full of wisdom, and perfect in beauty. He also operated as the covering angel, a highly prestigious position – he covered the throne of God (Ezekiel 28:11-19). He let his prominent status delude him into believing he could dethrone the Divine Deity and usurp God's sovereign position. (Isaiah 14:12). With his high position and next-to-perfect features and attributes, he managed to influence and convince one-third of the angels to follow him in his rebellion against the Almighty (Revelation 12:3-9). Upon his rebellion, Isaiah 14:12 says Lucifer was cast down to the earth. His presence in the Garden of Eden in the form of a serpent lends credence to this statement (Genesis 3).

In Ephesians 2:2, the apostle Paul gives us further information about Lucifer, now called Satan, by referring to him as the "prince of the power of the air." This tells us that although no longer occupying his great position of power in heaven, he can still manipulate and exert much influence over the airwaves and anything related to the air. Scripture makes no mention of Satan ever being cast into hell or of him ever being there, period.

With this understanding, I want you to consider that the "everlasting fire," "lake of fire," or "hell," was created as a place of judgment for Satan and the fallen angels (Matthew 25:41).

This is not a place where Satan or evil spirits rule or live, but instead, it is a place of torment reserved for them and they want to avoid it at all cost. We see proof of this in Matthew 8, when Jesus encountered two demon-possessed men and the evil spirits cried out, "Son of God, leave us alone! Have you come here to torment us before the time? Then the demons begged him, 'If you drive us out, send us into the herd of pigs,'" (Matthew 8:29; 31). The demons did not want Christ to cast them to hell and be tormented, which they knew would be their final destination and judgment. They also know that God has designated an appointed time and day for that.

This explains why the erroneous suppositions about sending Satan "back" to the pit hold no merit. We can also dismiss the notion regarding people in hell being tormented by demons. How could this be when demons have never been there, or desire to go there?

They know that they would be tormented there, as well.

Instead, it is biblical to believe that Satan and every evil spirit shudder in fear at the thought of that place. So the idea of binding Satan and banishing him back to the pit he came from, cannot be taken seriously. Even Jesus refused to make use of such an approach; he never cast a demon into hell but simply commanded the evil spirits to come out of a person, or in the case we read in Matthew 8, at the demons' plea, he cast them into the pigs (Matthew 8:32).

For those still believing that Satan or his demons continuously torment people in hell, there still remains this obvious question: how could they have taken over a place God created as a place of judgment for them? The answer is, they didn't. We can, however, read in the book of Revelation that at the end of the story, the dragon, the old-serpent, Satan, does finally end up in hell (Revelation 20)!

It is the progressive study of the Word of God that puts everything in its right perspective. When we approach spiritual matters without the accurate and proper counsel of Scripture, we will ourselves create questions and contradictions that don't exist.

I, too, have believed the testimonies of highly-regarded Christians who said God allowed them to visit hell; whether in a vision or a dream, they claimed to be first-hand witnesses of the sufferings and torment inflicted on those present at the hands of demons. These moving and compelling accounts inspired fear in their many listeners who heard of the imminent judgment that await those who refuse to believe and serve Christ. But regardless of the good intentions behind these erroneous testimonies and their subsequent books, we must always be able to answer this question, what does the Bible say? From even the few verses we just read, the Bible does not support such claims.

So the goal of this chapter involves each reader being able to clearly identify the effective methods determined by God to bring us great success in the face of an enemy who is like a roaring lion seeking who he can devour (2 Peter 5:8).

The True Meaning of 2 Corinthians 10:3-6

Many Christians frequently use Second Corinthians 10:3-6 for the purposes of spiritual warfare. The passage reads as follows:

> For though we walk in the flesh, we do not war after the flesh: (For the weapons of our warfare are not carnal, but mighty through God to the pulling down of strong holds;) Casting down imaginations, and every high thing that exalts itself against the knowledge of God, and bringing into captivity every thought to the obedience of Christ; And having in a readiness to revenge all disobedience, when your obedience is fulfilled. (AKJ)

This Scripture has often been recited during passionate prayers with the intention of speaking into the atmosphere and pulling down what may be perceived as strongholds in the spiritual realm. Such prayers typically lead to a series of rebukes and commands to Satan to loosen his grip on the place or thing that the person praying perceives Satan has a firm hold on. Let's consider some context to the verse to arrive to its intended conclusion, as a text without context is simply pretext.

God called the apostle Paul to minister to the Gentiles, or non-Jews, letting them know redemption was also available to them through Jesus Christ. Previously, the belief system of that time stated that salvation belonged only to the Jews, but Christ's ultimate sacrifice made salvation available for all who believed, regardless of who they were, where they came from, or what sins they had committed.

Paul spread this message with the same zeal and passion he had demonstrated in the Jewish beliefs he once held dear, to the point that he became the recipient of much of the same kind of physical persecution he once inflicted on Christians. In regard to his teachings, he faced opposition from the Jews, whose beliefs he abandoned; and because he persecuted Christians at one time, he also faced skepticism from Christians. To make matters worse, the church he founded in Corinth, started questioning his apostolic authority. It appears that a false teacher had, during Paul's absence, sowed seeds of doubt into the congregation at Corinth, inciting them to question Paul's apostolic calling and the messages he preached. It was this concern that Paul responded to in 2 Corinthians 10:1-2:

> *Now, I, Paul, appeal to you personally by the meekness and gentleness of Christ (I who am meek when present among you, but am full of courage toward you when away!) – Now I ask that when I am present I may not have to be bold with the confidence that (I expect) I will dare to use against some who consider us to be behaving according to human standards. (NET)*

The first two verses of this chapter give us insight into some of the specific criticisms Paul's agitators directed towards him. Apparently, Paul's critics complained about the assertive tone in his letters to them while he appeared much more timid in person. Recall, however, that Paul at one time persecuted Christians before his conversion. At the time, he had the authority to authorize their killings, and aggressively located Christians in order to do so. He certainly had no problem being bold or assertive! However, he referenced "the meekness and gentleness of Christ" in his attempt to make them see the transformation that had taken place in his life since his conversion. In verse two, he reaffirmed his authority as an apostle and his desire to not exercise it unless absolutely necessary. Again, these first two verses help us understand the context of Paul's response to those casting aspersions at him and his ministry; he didn't see the need to address Satan or the evil spirits. Second Corinthians 10:3-5 follows:

> *For though we live as human beings, we do not wage war according to human standards, for the weapons of our warfare are not human weapons, but are made powerful by God for*

tearing down strongholds. We tear down arguments and every arrogant obstacle that is raised up against the knowledge of God, and we take every thought captive to make it obey Christ.

Here Paul differentiated his approach and purpose from that of the carnal-minded. His motives did not center on the things that appeal to a secular mindset, such as material possessions, servants, or fame; the apostle didn't rely on the natural weapons or methods commonly used to obtain such things. Instead, his goal focused on converting his listeners to Christ, so he resorted to divine and spiritual weapons that could overcome the obstacles standing in the way of his objective. These included strongholds, or erroneous belief systems, arguments, thoughts, perspectives and ideas that kept people from the knowledge of God and from becoming converted. The only weapons powerful enough to accomplish this were the gospel message and a lifestyle that provided proof of its truth by its holy fruit. This combination consistently penetrated the hearts of listeners, and inclined their will, emotions, and intellect toward the true and living God and towards his way of salvation.

A wrong perspective of strongholds I once held

The fiery church I grew up in taught me that the strongholds referred to in 2 Corinthians 10:4 referred to bondages, or spiritual chains, that Satan imposed on individuals against their will. Such bondages over which they had no control included drugs, alcohol and any other type of addictions that could only be broken by rebuking them in Jesus' name; fasting and anointing people and their apparel also seemed to do the work in the more extreme cases. However, when looking at the Greek word for "strongholds" in this verse, you'll find that the word *ochuroma*, means "castle" or "bondage" and not "chains." The concept of willfully using a castle or fortress as a mode of defense comes into play here as it did when kings from the past did when being attacked.

Symbolically, *ochuroma* means "an argument or a philosophical reasoning." One dictionary defines it as "any argument or reasoning relied upon by which the disputant endeavors to fortify his opinion, defending it against his opponent" – in this case, human reasoning against the knowledge of God.

Paul refers to the strongholds mentioned in this verse as belief systems that kept people from knowing the true God; these varying doctrines included teachings from pagan religions, Greek philosophy, Judaism, and false teachers. And like a fortress that's capable of protecting anyone inside it with its impenetrable walls from those on the outside, erroneous belief systems people hold dearly can be just as powerful in keeping people from knowing God. The false teachings and arguments of Paul's time strove to keep people from the knowledge of the true God. Paul's message to the Corinthians assured them that the Gospel of Jesus Christ always wins, even against the strongholds alluded to in 2 Corinthians 10:4. The fact that many in this church abandoned their pagan lifestyles to serve the living God demonstrates the power of the gospel against any demonic influences.

Paul declared the gospel message and a lifestyle of holiness that bears the fruit of its truth, to be the only effective weapons in advancing against the enemy's strongholds. Again, strongholds are beliefs that keep people from knowing and surrendering to God. So, why does Satan determine to keep us ignorant as to what true strongholds are and how to overcome them? Because by doing so, our focus would be diverted to activities and methods that do not bring about any heavenly transformation, such as, shouting rebukes at Satan and his strongholds. Satan prefers that the body of Christ engages him in ineffective methods, as opposed to effective methods like the truth of the gospel message and the word of God. And if we were confident that only the gospel message contains the power and ability to tear down all arguments that keep people from God, we would commit ourselves to the diligent study of the Scriptures, and Satan wants to avoid that at all costs. He prefers for people to believe, among other things, that their authority and anointing cause strongholds to be broken, he knows it's not true – that outlook only exalts man and suppresses the majesty of Christ – the one to whom all authority and dominion was given. Or he prefers to hoodwink Christians into believing that prayer alone will penetrate people's erroneous beliefs and somehow come to a realization about the true God on their own. While something like this occurring might be considered miraculous, the truth remains that simply praying about false beliefs produces little difference. People need an experience with the gospel message, as without it, the strongholds will likely remain.

The Meaning of Binding and Loosing

Some may contend that Matthew 16:13-20 gives Christians authority to bind strongholds or loose people from them. Let's look at this passage of Scripture closely to determine what it really says:

> *When Jesus came to the area of Caesarea Philippi, he asked his disciples, "Who do people say that the Son of Man is?" They answered, "Some say John the Baptist, others Elijah, and others Jeremiah or one of the prophets." He said to them, "But who do you say that I am?" Simon Peter answered, "You are the Christ, the Son of the living God." And Jesus answered him, "You are blessed, Simon son of Jonah, because flesh and blood did not reveal this to you, but my Father in heaven!*
>
> *And I tell you that you are Peter, and on this rock I will build my church, and the gates of Hades will not overpower it. I will give you the keys of the kingdom of heaven. Whatever you bind on earth will have been bound in heaven, and whatever you release on earth will have been released in heaven." Then he instructed his disciples not to tell anyone that he was the Christ.*

When interpreting Scripture, we must consider several aspects of a passage, including the setting, audience, culture, and time period. The occasion in the above texts occurred in Caesarea Philippi, at the base of Mount Hermon, the place where in Old Testament times, King Jeroboam of Israel led God's people into idolatry. Greatly influenced by Greek mythology, this place became the center of worship of the Greek god, Pan, during the time of Christ.

A half-human-half-goat god of the wild, shepherds and hunters, Pan acted as a symbol of lust and wild sexual perversions. Classical writings also refer to him as a "seer," or fortuneteller, and a giver of revelations. The many shrines built in Pan's honor at Caesera Philippi demonstrated the people's commitment to this "god." These shrines could be found at the base of the mountain. There also existed an enormous spring of water the people called Panias, in Pan's honor. Considered to be a bottomless pit because of its size, abundance, and immeasurable depth, it also functioned as the water source for the Jordan River.

Legend has it, that both the cave and the body of water were considered to be gateways to the underworld. The people of the time believed that Pan went to rest in the underworld during the winter. His worshipers engaged in despicable, sexual acts, including sex with goats, in order to please him enough to ensure his return the next spring.

By committing such acts, the people were "knocking" on the gates of hell, or Hades, or the "unseen" world, hoping that Pan would respond favorably.

So why would Christ choose such an abominable place to reveal himself as the Messiah to his disciples and go over, again, his plans to build a church? Christ chose this place to use a popular pagan god and location as a prop to effectively and powerfully make a resounding statement to his disciples and to the kingdom of darkness.

Notice how he symbolically used aspects of Pan and the location to make his point. First, our heavenly Father outshone Pan's fabricated epiphanies by disclosing the greatest revelation of all to Simon, son of Jonas - Jesus, the Messiah, Son of the living God!

This was the work of the real God providing real revelation.

Furthermore, Christ communicated with his disciples in the Aramaic language. In verse 17, Christ addressed Peter by his birth name, Simon Barjona, in order to create distinction from his God-given name and function, in verse 18, of Peter, or Cephas in Aramaic. Cephas is pronounced kay-fas, meaning "the Rock." Cephas has an Aramaic origin of kafe, meaning "a hollow rock!"

The famous cave, which is also a hollow in a rock, in Caesarea Philippi, at the base of Mount Hermon, was the place where the followers of Pan gathered for worship and to receive revelations from Pan; and Peter, or Cephas, would also be the hollow of a rock where the church, or "called out ones," would be gathered together through his gospel message – the revelation of the divine mystery! Again, it would be through the "hollow rock," Peter, that God would also provide the divine revelation of the Son of God as Messiah, and the gospel message!

When Christ emphatically stated that the "Gates of hell would not prevail" against the Church, he meant the powers of the unseen world. Gates symbolized the strength of a city; and hell, or Hades, meant the "unseen" world.

Once he made that clear, Christ went on to further inform Peter that he would be given the keys to the kingdom. Well, what do keys do? They open doors! On the day of Pentecost, what occurred? God used Peter to establish his church as he opened the door to the kingdom of God through the preaching of the divine revelation. Peter shared Jesus as the Messiah and proclaimed that Christ was sent by God to make reconciliation between God and man possible through his death and resurrection; by grace through faith in Jesus, both Jews and Gentiles could become part of that Kingdom.

Symbolically, keys also signify "authority" and this explains why Christ told Peter, "Whatever you bind on earth will be bound in heaven, and whatever you loose on earth will be loosed in heaven." However, this statement had nothing to do with the Lord's earlier assertion, "…and the gates of hell will not prevail against it." Partnering these two Scriptures gives way to erroneous teachings.

Matthew 16:19 illustrates the use of a popular Jewish idiom much like the English colloquialisms popular in our culture. When we say, "It's raining cats and dogs," we know that cats and dogs don't fall from the sky; the idiom paints a picture of abundant rain. Well, the Jews frequently spoke of binding and loosing as an idiom for declaring something lawful or unlawful; the term likewise alludes to granting or withholding permission, allowing or not allowing something to take place.

In the early days of the church, God used Peter and the apostles to establish its ordinances. He gave them the authority to determine those things that would be allowed or forbidden, lawful and unlawful. Acts 15:22-29 provides us with an example of this.

> *Then the apostles and elders, with the whole church, decided to send men chosen from among them, Judas called Barsabbas and Silas, leaders among the brothers, to Antioch with Paul and Barnabas. They sent this letter with them: From the apostles and elders, your brothers, to the Gentile brothers and sisters in Antioch, Syria, and Cilicia, greetings! Since we have heard that some have gone out from among us with no orders from us and have confused you, upsetting your minds by what they said, we have unanimously decided to choose men to send to you along with our dear friends Barnabas and Paul, who have risked their lives for the name of our Lord Jesus Christ. Therefore we are sending Judas and Silas who will tell you these things themselves in person. For it seemed best to the Holy Spirit and to us not to place any greater burden on you than these necessary rules: that you abstain from meat that has been sacrificed to idols and from blood and from what has been strangled and from sexual immorality. If you keep yourselves from doing these things, you will do well. Farewell.*

As you can see, they forbade sexual immorality, eating food that had been sacrificed to idols, and eating meat from an animal that had been strangled or that still had blood in it. Furthermore, in Acts chapter 10, warned against interfering with God's decision to baptize the Gentiles with the Holy Spirit, Peter deemed the conversion of non-Jews as acceptable. Again, what do we see in these examples? God had given authority to the apostles to lay the foundational teachings and regulations for the newly formed church, and they further did it in the epistles they authored.

To further clarify the misconception that "binding and loosing" refers to evil spirits or Satan, let's look at Matthew 18:15-22.

> *"If your brother sins, go and show him his fault when the two of you are alone. If he listens to you, you have regained your brother. But if he does not listen, take one or two others with you, so that at the testimony of two or three witnesses every matter may be established. If he refuses to listen to them, tell it to the church. If he refuses to listen to the church, treat him like a Gentile or a tax collector."*

> *"I tell you the truth, whatever you bind on earth will have been bound in heaven, and whatever you release on earth will have been released in heaven. Again, I tell you the truth, if two of you on earth agree about whatever you ask, my Father in heaven will do it for you. For where two or three are assembled in my name, I am there among them."* Then Peter came to him and said, *"Lord, how many times must I forgive my brother who sins against me? As many as seven times?"* Jesus said to him, *"Not seven times, I tell you, but seventy-seven times!*

This passage has nothing to do with evil spirits, but instead, the process Christians should use when attempting to restore another Christian who has sinned against them and caused injury by word or conduct.

After establishing this process, Christ put his seal of approval on this method for restoring fractured Christian relationships by using the Jewish idom, "Whatever you bind...Whatever you loose..." Again, this Jewish idiom had nothing really to do with binding or loosing evil spirits or Satan, but rather of establishing something as permissible or forbidden.

A Closer Look at the Armor of God

Many Bible teachers also use Ephesians 6:10-17 when teaching about spiritual warfare:

> *Finally, be strengthened in the Lord and in the strength of his power. Clothe yourselves with the armor of God so that you may be able to stand against the schemes of the devil. For our struggle is not against flesh and blood, but against the rulers, against the powers, against the world of rulers of this darkness, against the spiritual forces of evil in the heavens. For this reason, take up the full armor of God so that you may be able to stand your ground on the evil day, and having done everything, to stand. Stand firm therefore, by fastening the belt of truth around your waist, by putting on the breastplate of righteousness, by fitting your feet with the preparation that comes from the good news of peace, and in all of this, by taking up the shield of faith with which you can extinguish all the flaming arrows of the evil one. And take the helmet of salvation and the sword of the Spirit, which is the word of God.*

The focus in many circles of Christianity centers on our struggles against a spiritual realm, ruled by Satan or the dark powers of the unseen world. Again, Satan DOES NOT want the Kingdom of God to advance and uses every weapon at his disposal to prevent that from happening; he REALLY likes to lure Christians away from their faith! Before taking a closer look at the apostle Paul's formula for standing against Satan's vicious attacks, we need to direct our attention to the word "finally" at the beginning of this passage; it indicates an earlier dialogue leading up to his final instructions. We would be wise to consider the content of those instructions before his final thoughts, as it may add value to our understanding of his final counsel to the church in Ephesus.

In short, herein are the exhortations Paul wrote in the passages that lead up to Ephesians 6:10. In chapter four, he encouraged the church to *live in unity* and *to live holy lives*. In chapter five, he reminded the church to *live in love, in the light,* and *to live wisely*. Then, toward the end of that chapter he instructed the church's husbands and wives how to *live out a marriage that pleased God*. He then described what a God honoring relationship looked like between parents and children, and employees and employers. As you can see, the chapters and verses that lead up to Ephesians 6:10 are exhortations for Christians to live lives that display the fruit of their conversion; this includes bearing the fruit of conversion in every relationship. In short, Paul was admonishing Christians to live in such a way that clearly demonstrates the transforming power of God's grace in their lives.

However, many have failed to pay heed to Paul's counsel that leads up to Ephesians 6:10-20, instead focusing heavily on the realm of the invisible by "attacking" forces of darkness through spiritual rituals they've developed. From their perspective, the "more anointed," "more spiritual" and "more mature" someone is, the more they will be inclined, and even called, to "war" against forces of darkness in the spiritual world, mostly with demand-filled, verbal assaults against Satan and evil spirits.

The truth is, if we don't bear fruit in the practical aspects of our lives, we will usually succumb to the schemes of the devil mentioned in Ephesians 6:10. We cannot think that living righteously and bearing fruit in our practical lives and relationships is not being spiritual. To the contrary, that's about as spiritual as one can get! A righteous lifestyle that testifies we have been washed in the atoning blood of Jesus and brought to life from spiritual death is absolutely spiritual and evidence that we are winning in spiritual warfare!

Since we now realize that Satan wishes to shipwreck every facet of our lives, and ultimately, our faith, we need to put on the armor of God. This enables us to withstand the enemy's attacks in a manner that will not negatively reflect on our lives as believers but protect the fruit of our salvation.

Because some people may think that the armor refers to their anointing, calling, spiritual covering or authority, pay close attention to what Scripture defines as the armor of God, as it will tell us differently.

Paul makes it clear that the seven things that cause us to stand against Satan and the powers of darkness that influence this world are: the belt of **Truth**, the breastplate of **Righteousness**, the **Gospel Message**, the shield of **Faith**, the helmet of **Salvation**, the sword of the Spirit which is the **Word of God**, and **Praying in the Spirit**.

When I understood the Scriptures less thoroughly, I thought God wanted me to stand against Satan, and even advance against his kingdom, by rebuking the devil, shouting demands at him with authority, and making accusations against him before God.

I truly believed I had the upper hand when I started binding the spirits of darkness and loosening their hold on the atmosphere and on the people I may have been praying for. To my surprise, the Scriptures I thought supported such practices actually didn't. In fact, the Bible does not support such actions, or even imply Christians should do them.

Satan absolutely delighted in my ignorant and ineffective efforts to defeat him. When I began to comprehend his schemes and God's instructions for warfare, I could finally embrace and put into use the full armor of God. None of the armor of God mentions "my authority in God," "my anointing," "my gifts" or "call," or anything of the like. Instead, notice how the armor of God proves effective against Satan's schemes.

Cunning and crafty, Satan can only lie and deceive, therefore, the belt of *truth*, or simply put, *truth*, exposes him and his lies, thus preventing a person from falling for his deceptions.

The breastplate of righteousness is mentioned next. There is no greater witness that validates the work of God in our lives than righteousness. It is the banner that rises high and proclaims that we are the handiwork of God and have been transformed! Paul illustrates it as a breastplate, the part of a soldier's armor that covers the heart. Righteousness covers and protects our heart with holiness, integrity, purity, and sincerity. These characteristics help defuse fiery arrows of temptation that Satan tries to derail us with. While emotionally charged rebukes appear more sensational and appear to be more spiritual, they fall short in comparison to the defense against Satan's schemes that a heart covered in righteousness can provide.

Interestingly, the sandals worn by the Roman and Greek soldiers, whom Paul frequently alluded to, came with spikes that gave them better traction so they could avoid falling or slipping. They came equipped with greaves or boots made of brass to protect the ankles and legs (shins). These helped ward off any injuries to their lower extremities that might prevent them from standing or advancing forward. Paul helps the Christian reader to understand how all the virtues and truth found in the gospel protect our footing; it allows us to walk the Christian life with a firm grip on Christ, our foundation, without stumbling. An onslaught of rebukes or pleading the blood will never accomplish this - only the gospel of Christ can do that!

Furthermore, Paul taught the Christians in Ephesus that faith, like a shield, extinguished Satan's fiery arrows of temptation. In looking at Jesus' conversation with Peter in (Luke 22:31), he taught us the same concept. In the verse cited, Jesus informed Simon Peter that Satan desired to sift him as wheat. Had the practice of rebuking Satan been one that Christ sought to establish for his followers as an effective way to stand against Satan, that moment would have been a perfect time to do so; however, he didn't. Instead, he informed Peter that he prayed for him that his faith would not fail (Luke 22:32)! Why?

The fact is that faith, or our conviction and persuasion about the Son of God, is powerful enough to extinguish any schemes of Satan designed to derail us. Our confidence in Christ keeps us pressing forward in the way of righteousness. Recall what happened to Peter after his conversation with Jesus in Luke 22, on the night of Christ's arrest. When asked if he knew Jesus, he denied him three separate times. After the third denial, the rooster crowed just as Christ predicted. Peter, then faced the realization that he had not only betrayed his Savior but also his friend.

In Luke 22:62, we learn that after Peter denied Christ three times and the rooster crowed, "…he went outside and wept bitterly." While his courage failed him when it came to the test, his faith did not. Experiencing deep remorse because of his convictions about Christ's identity, he began to weep earnestly in repentance! This allowed God to raise him back up and advance the kingdom of God.

Additionally, Paul referenced the helmet of salvation to encourage the believers that the hope of our salvation would protect and preserve our minds in the midst of Satan's attacks. He stressed the importance of protecting our minds as it functions as the control center for our will, emotions, and decisions. Christ's eventual return should fortify our minds plus keep us steadfast in our faith and the hope of our salvation. The hope of being totally restored to God should infuse us with courage during times of hardships, trials, and tribulation, and that ought to be able to keep us from falling away.

For offense, God has placed in our hands the sword of the Spirit, otherwise known as the Word of God. Interestingly, no other tool found in the armor of God can be used for offense in warfare. Satan prefers to have us yell, rebuke, attempt to cast him out, and even sing songs like, "Satan is Under My Feet," as long as we don't declare the truths of the Word of God and loudly proclaim its gospel message. Again, only this method makes it possible to advance against Satan and his kingdom!

Attempting to gain ground on Satan by any other means is folly, and will, ultimately, result in defeat. Our call, anointing, gift, church titles, experience, background, connections, spiritual coverings, church membership, associations, or any other thing to the like, is ineffective against Satan – only the truth of the Word of God will prevail.

Paul continued to give the church instruction on how to effectively stand against Satan in verses 18-20.

> *With every prayer and petition, pray at all times in the Spirit, and to this end be alert, with all perseverance and requests for all the saints. Pray for me also, that I may be given the message when I begin to speak – that I may confidently make known the mystery of the gospel, for which I am an ambassador in chains. Pray that I may be able to speak boldly as I ought to speak.*

Paul exhorted the church to pray in the Spirit at all times. He did not mean to actually pray in tongues as this verse has often been interpreted. In fact, praying in the Spirit closely parallels walking in the Spirit.

You see, walking in the Spirit does not mean speaking in tongues wherever we go. It simply means walking in the will and the desire of the Spirit of God. Therefore, Paul exhorted the church in Ephesus to also pray in the Spirit, making full use of this marvelous gift that allows us to pray the perfect will of the Father. God only commits to answering those prayers that align with his will and desire.

An example of this type of prayer was Paul's request to the Ephesians to pray for him to confidently make known the mystery of the gospel – the message of Reconciliation! Making known the mystery of the gospel message is still the will of God for us today, and the only message effective in advancing the kingdom of God!

The Christian's Obligation in Warfare

Satan, however, delights when we stay in ignorance in regard to the Word of God. In fact, he scoffs at our rebukes because he knows that we were never given authority to rebuke him. Zechariah 3:1-7 further highlights this point.

> *Next I saw Joshua the high priest standing before the angel of the LORD, with Satan standing at his right hand to accuse him. The LORD said to Satan, "May the LORD rebuke you, Satan! May the LORD, who has chosen Jerusalem, rebuke you! Isn't this man like a burning stick snatched from the fire?" Now Joshua was dressed in filthy clothes as he stood there before the angel. The angel spoke up to those standing all around, "Remove his filthy clothes." Then he said to Joshua, "I have freely forgiven your iniquity and will dress you in fine clothing." Then I spoke up, "Let a clean turban be put on his head." So they put a clean turban on his head and clothed him, while the angel of the LORD stood nearby. Then the angel of the LORD exhorted Joshua solemnly: "The LORD who rules over all says, 'If you live and work according to my requirements, you will be able to preside over my temple and attend to my courtyards, and I will allow you to come and go among these others who are standing by you.*

God gave this vision to Zechariah to offer encouragement for the Jews continuing to rebuild the temple. This took place after 70 years of Babylonian captivity when the Jews were "snatched out of the fire," as the angel of the Lord so eloquently put it.

While their adversaries attempted to stop their work, Satan launched his own attack in the spirit realm, accusing them before

God of the sins that led to their captivity. In God's vision to Zechariah, Satan stood before the angel of the Lord accusing Joshua, the high priest, a symbol of the Jewish people; even the angel of the Lord refrained from rebuking Satan, and never instructed Joshua to turn to his accuser and rebuke him.

Instead, the angel of the Lord left the rebuking to the One most qualified to do it – God himself!

The angel of the Lord issued the orders to remove Joshua's filthy garments, which were a symbol of sin, and replace them with fine clothes; the fine clothes symbolized the righteousness freely given to him as his sins had been removed, or forgiven. The angel proceeded to exhort Joshua to live and walk according to God's requirements.

Essentially, God used this vision to exhort his people to live holy lives because of the right standing with God freely given to them.

This passage clearly emphasizes that those forgiven of their sins need not dispute, rebuff, or rebuke Satan; instead, they needed to focus on keeping their garments clean, a symbol of righteousness, by not falling back into sin. As for Satan, it was God's responsibility to rebuke him. In fact, a designated day has already been set when God will completely destroy him.

In like manner, we, as Christians, must make every effort to take care of the fine clothing or righteousness that Christ has clothed us with when He redeemed us and "snatched us out of the fire," the bondage of sin and eternal damnation. God wants us to focus on our walk and ensure that we don't fall back into a lifestyle of sin so that we can enjoy access into his presence and be ready when Christ returns. Satan, on the other hand, would prefer we focus on him so that we would lose sight of our walk.

Now, some may contend that a story from the Old Testament lacks the authority bestowed on believers in the New Testament. They may argue that we have the power to rebuke the devil himself. (Remember not to confuse the casting out of evil spirits, as in Mark 6:13, or submission of demons, as in Luke 10:17-20, with the rebuking of Satan - those are totally different). Jude verses 3-13, in the New Testament, addresses the issue of rebuking Satan:

Dear friends, although I have been eager to write to you about our common salvation, I now feel compelled instead to write to encourage you to contend earnestly for the faith that was once for all entrusted to the saints. For certain men have secretly slipped in among you—men who long ago were marked out for the condemnation I am about to describe—ungodly men who have turned the grace of our God into a license for evil and who deny our only Master and Lord, Jesus Christ.

Now I desire to remind you (even though you have been fully informed of these facts once for all) that Jesus, having saved the people out of the land of Egypt, later destroyed those who did not believe. You also know that the angels who did not keep within their proper domain but abandoned their own place of residence, he has kept in eternal chains in utter darkness, locked up for the judgment of the great Day. So also Sodom and Gomorrah and the neighboring towns, since they indulged in sexual immorality and pursued unnatural desire in a way similar to these angels, are now displayed as an example by suffering the punishment of eternal fire. Yet these men, as a result of their dreams, defile the flesh, reject authority, and insult the glorious ones. But even when Michael the archangel was arguing with the devil and debating with him concerning Moses' body, he did not dare to bring a slanderous judgment, but said, "May the Lord rebuke you!" But these men do not understand the things they slander, and they are being destroyed by the very things that, like irrational animals, they instinctively comprehend. Woe to them! For they have traveled down Cain's path, and because of greed have abandoned themselves to Balaam's error; hence, they will certainly perish in Korah's rebellion. These men are dangerous reefs at your love feasts,

feasting without reverence, feeding only themselves. They are
waterless clouds, carried along by the winds; autumn trees
without fruit—twice dead, uprooted; wild sea waves, spew-
ing out the foam of their shame; wayward stars for whom the
utter depths of eternal darkness have been reserved.

Jude found the occasion in which Michael the Archangel con-
tended over the body of Moses and refrained from slandering Satan still applicable under the new covenant. Even Jude understood
that the act of rebuking Satan only belonged to the Lord.

Conclusion

We must continue to keep in mind the enmity that exists between
God and his archenemy, Satan. God has been working throughout time to once and for all, completely do away with sin and the
devil. Because of our limited comprehension and ability, our Creator cannot allow us to tackle this job.

To sum it up, God wants Christians to guard the righteousness he
freely clothed us with by his grace. We must continue to submit to
the Spirit's work of sanctification in our lives. Finally, we need to
contend for the faith, using the shield that helps us stand effectively
against Satan.

The weight of Scripture suggests that we overcome Satan as Christ
did, which guarantees us our victory. A closer examination of Christ's
victory over Satan reveals that Jesus never once rebuked or even addressed the devil while on the Cross. One would think that somewhere in the midst of the Lord's last seven utterances, he would make
at least one comment warning Satan of his upcoming defeat. He
never did. How then could he defeat Satan and never even address
or mention him? It was by virtue of obedience to the will and commands of God that Jesus overcame and defeated Satan! Revelation
12:10-11 conveys the same idea!

Then I heard a loud voice in heaven saying, "The salvation and the power and the kingdom of our God, and ruling authority of his Christ, have now come, because the accuser of our brothers and sisters, the one who accuses them day and night before our God, has been thrown down. But they overcame him by the blood of the Lamb and by the word of their testimony, and they did not love their lives so much that they were afraid to die."

Did you catch that? For Christians, we overcome Satan by virtue of the forgiveness granted to us by the shed blood of Jesus and by the word of our testimony. What does "the word of their testimony" mean? It means the testimony our lifestyles give of our conversion, a lifestyle that shows the fruit of our transformation – holiness – obedience to God's will, Word, and commands! Testimony in this verse does not refer to verbal testimony as much as it does to the witness of God our righteous lives convey!

Finally, let us, like Paul, experience success as we remain faithful to God's strategies; to achieve his will in our lives, in our fight against spiritual darkness. In his first epistle to the Thessalonians, Paul told the church, "For we wanted to come to you – certainly I, Paul, did, again and again – but Satan blocked our way," (2:18, NIV). How did he respond to Satan's hindrance? Rebuke? Mysticism? Not at all! Instead, a more effective strategy – "We sent Timothy, our brother and fellow worker for God in the gospel of Christ, to strengthen you and encourage you about your faith," (3:2, NET).

The strategy is clear: receive forgiveness through the blood of Christ and guard the righteousness he clothed you with; continue to maintain the holy lifestyle that the spirit has called you to live. Pay heed to God's teachings and resist Satan's assaults through the virtues represented by the armor of God in Ephesians. Spread the message of the gospel of Jesus Christ at all cost. When Satan works to hinder the advancement of the gospel, be persistent, and find another way to advance it. And lastly, rejoice, because as Paul wrote in Romans 16:20, "The God of peace will soon crush Satan under your feet," (NLT). God will rebuke Satan for you and has designated a day when the enemy of our God and faith will be cast into the lake of fire and destroyed forever.

CONCLUSION

We have come to the end of this book, but with much prayer, you will begin a new chapter in your life. I pray that you caught the message of reconciliation, sanctification, and restoration found in Nehemiah's reconstruction of Jerusalem's walls and gates. I also hope you came to understand that this is the intended purpose God has for your life and for all of humanity. This message will serve to take away our trouble and disgrace before God and allows us the great privilege of being reconciled to him and partake in the hope of being totally restored to him at Christ's return.

This book does not cover the last two gates mentioned in Nehemiah 3, the East Gate and the Gate of Inspection. They serve to herald God's amazing conclusion to his master plan of restoration at Christ's Second Coming and the Final Judgment of all mankind. These two gates lead us to the study of end-times and the understanding of end-time prophecy. If you desire to learn more about the subject matter of the final two gates, please read the excellent material by Dr. Franklin Fowler, Director of Prophecy Research Initiative, who has committed a large part of his life to studying and writing about end-time prophecy in great detail. His comprehensive work found online at endtimeissues.com, will definitely provide you with great clarity and understanding on this vital subject. Dr. Fowler's study material goes much further in-depth than what you would find in most common end-time material and information typically studied today.

For now, I pray that you have been both inspired and burdened to embrace God's plan for reconciliation and sanctification as never before, and have gained a passion to restore this message in the many sectors of the Church that have abandoned it. Remember to leverage this book as a map to help you understand where you are along the journey in God's predestined path set for every Christian. Let it encourage and inspire you to persevere to the end.

Thank you for investing time in reading this book. If it has been a blessing to you, share a copy with someone, and most importantly, promote God's divine message summarized in 2 Corinthians 5:17-21 and Titus 2:11-14:

> *Therefore, if anyone is in Christ, the new creation has come: The old has gone, the new is here! All this is from God, who reconciled us to himself through Christ and gave us the ministry of reconciliation: that God was reconciling the world to himself in Christ, not counting people's sins against them. And he has committed to us the message of reconciliation. We are therefore Christ's ambassadors, as though God were making his appeal through us. We implore you on Christ's behalf: Be reconciled to God. God made him who had no sin to be sin for us, so that in him we might become the righteousness of God. (NIV)*

> *For the grace of God has appeared that offers salvation to all people. It teaches us to say "No" to ungodliness and worldly passions, and to live self-controlled, upright and godly lives in this present age, while we wait for the blessed hope—the appearing of the glory of our great God and Savior, Jesus Christ, who gave himself for us to redeem us from all wickedness and to purify for himself a people that are his very own, eager to do what is good. (NIV)"*